MW00635183

Bob —
Enjoy!

Jerry Ferguson
SEPT '08

Lean
Administration

An Organization's Journey to Implement Lean as a System

Lean
Administration

An Organization's Journey to Implement Lean as a System

by
Jerry Feingold

WCM Associates LLC
Fort Wayne, IN
www.wcmfg.com

Lean Administration: An Organization's Journey to Implement
Lean as a System

By Jerry Feingold

Copyright 2008 Jerry Feingold.
All rights reserved.
Printed in the United States of America

No part of this book may be reproduced or utilized in any form or
by any means, electronic or mechanical, including photocopying,
recording, or by any information storage and retrieval system
without the permission of the publisher. Address all inquiries to:

WCM Associates LLC
P.O. Box 8035
Fort Wayne, IN   46898-8035
(260)637-8064
www.wcmfg.com

Disclaimer

Demonstrations and illustrations contained herein provide only a
description of general improvement techniques and methods.
Illustrations and directions may not provide all necessary or
relevant information and the authors suggest that you refer to
appropriate equipment manuals specific to the particular task or
contact a qualified craftsman or professional. By purchasing this
book and not immediately returning it after reviewing this
disclaimer, you agree that the authors may not be held responsible
for any omissions or inaccuracies in any information provided
herein.

ISBN #978-0-9793331-1-8

Front and back cover design by:
Robert Aulucino, www.aulicinodesign.com

Book and text design by WCM Associates LLC

Printed and bound by:
Thomson-Shore, Inc.
Dexter, MI
(734)426-3939

Library of Congress Catalog Card Number: 2008931654

This is a work of fiction. Names, characters, places,
and incidents are either products of the author's imagination or are
used in a fictional manner. Any resemblance to actual events or
locales or persons, living or dead, is entirely coincidental.

This book is dedicated to those effective, wise, open-minded leaders who, in the words of Warren G. Bennis, "translate vision into reality." In my years in business I am amazed at how often I meet people in a leadership position who can't articulate their vision and are reluctant to embrace new paradigms, leaders who can come up with excuses for not trying something new. "Our business is different," "What you're proposing would only work in large enterprises," "My tyrannical CEO would never let me try something like this." I salute those of you with the courage to act and to embrace the need for continuous improvement.

I also dedicate this book to my wonderful wife Ruthann, and to Erik and Ellyn Feingold, my terrific children.

Acknowledgements

I would like to thank my publisher, Larry Rubrich, for working with me on this book. His suggestions on the content and organization were important in making it better. I was fortunate to find in Larry a very unusual combination. He is not only a successful publisher but also an experienced Lean business consultant.

I also say thank you to the business leaders who helped me write this book, in particular, John Convery, Paul Johnson, and Amy Grant.

A special word of recognition goes to Don Esters who has been a friend and mentor for over twenty years and who set me on my exciting senior executive path.

From the Publisher

Lean Administration: The Next Frontier for Companies Trying to become Globally Competitive

Industry Week magazine reported in its October 2006 edition that of the 801 companies that responded to their Census of Manufacturers survey, less than 2% reported that they had achieved World Class status as a result of strategic improvement practices (primarily Lean & Lean Sigma).

Many companies have used Lean/World Class Manufacturing techniques to make their production areas highly competitive, yet these same companies often still find themselves short of being able to compete globally, and therefore consider chasing the low wages of a foreign country. Why are these companies having trouble competing globally?

The answer to this question is that we must apply Lean in our organizations as a "system." The Lean Enterprise is what we need. The reasons we have not applied Lean as a system are noted below.

First, we have defined "adding value," an absolutely critical measure in Lean, in manufacturing terms. It is defined as "changing the shape or form of the product" or as "what the customer is willing to pay for." These both have manufacturing connotations. This is supported by the fact that many Value Stream Mapping books only consider the manufacturing operations when calculating the percent of value-added time. What about the cost (and impact on our lead-times) of the ten days the customer order spent in the administrative/engineering areas before it hit the shop floor?

Secondly, this manufacturing definition of adding value has led us to ignore the administrative function and its impact on overhead costs. Yet, can we produce a physical product in manufacturing without the "knowledge product" or "information product" known as the engineering drawing? Or without the customer order entered into our system, or without raw materials? Or could we produce a quality product without standard work?

The administrative areas of our companies do produce a product—not like the physical product we produce in manufacturing, but a knowledge or information product that supports the production of the physical product. Unfortunately, our Lean concentration in manufacturing and our lack of understanding of what products are produced in our office areas, have left us with administrative areas that are the least productive area of our companies.

Why are administrative areas the least productive part of our business? One reason: we don't do something in our administrative areas that we always do in manufacturing— measure! We know how many widgets all of our machines can produce in an hour, and how many widgets we can assemble and ship in a day, but we don't know how many information/ knowledge products (quotes, customer orders, new designs, work orders, part purchases, etc.) we can do in an hour or a day.

To understand how this affects a company's overall productivity, we must look at the pie chart shown in Figure #1.

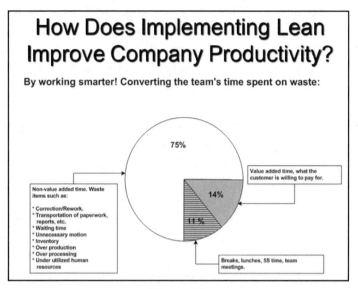

Figure #1

Figure #1 is a composite pie chart that represents a company video recording of two of its associates, one from the administrative area and one from the factory, for an entire day/ shift. The following day the videos are reviewed and what the associates did all day is categorized.

First, 11% of their day was spent on breaks, lunches, 5S time, and in team meetings. The company wants their associates doing these things, so the company is happy about this part of the pie.

Second, 14% of the day was spent on value-added time, doing things the customer is willing to pay for. If you showed this part of the video to the customer, they would say yes, that is what I'm paying you guys to do.

Third, 75% of the day was spent on non-value adding activities (waste), activities the customer is not willing to pay for. If the customer is not willing to pay for these activities, then the company must, and this money comes right out of profits. Remember, it's not that these people weren't busy during this 75%—they were—unfortunately, they were busy doing things the customer will not pay for.

If we broke down the 14% value added time into factory and administration percentages, we would find the factory percentage to be much higher (30%-40%) and the administrative area much lower (1%-5%).

To compete globally, we must continue to improve our manufacturing processes, and radically improve our administrative productivity by making sure the office is measuring/tracking their value added and non-value added parts of the pie.

As a company we would like our pie to look like Figure #2.

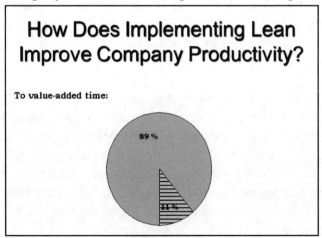

How Does Implementing Lean Improve Company Productivity?

To value-added time:

89 %

11 %

Figure #2

In his second Lean book, *Lean Administration*, Jerry Feingold does a great job of giving us an example of how most manufacturing organizations overlook their office/administrative functions as opportunities to improve their competiveness.

Sonic Labs, a manufacturer of loudspeakers, has implemented Lean only in their manufacturing area. The results for Sonic were great—reduced inventory and manufacturing costs, and a manufacturing lead-time reduced to 2 days.

Unfortunately, in the globally competitive business of loudspeaker manufacturing, this still left Sonic priced 20 percent higher than their foreign competition and with a total lead-time (administrative + manufacturing) of 70 days versus 45 days for the competition.

Instead of looking at how the Lean improvements that Sonic made in manufacturing might be applied to improve the "Sonic system efficiency," top management at Sonic panics and decides the only way to reduce its costs is to chase cheap labor and move the manufacturing to China (in typical U.S. business fashion). Sonic will fill its pipelines with inventory in an attempt to reduce its total lead-time.

Spurred by the belief of a Sonic manager that Lean needs to be applied in their organization as a system, this manager builds "Lean as a system" support by starting to apply Lean in the administrative area through the use of kaizen events.

Jerry Feingold skillfully completes this story of Sonic's journey to implement Lean as a system and Sonic's discovery of how this impacts their ability to compete globally.

Introduction

Most books about Lean focus on manufacturing. Typical techniques presented in these books deal with subjects like assembly line balancing and setup time reduction. Many manufacturing companies initiate Lean in the factory and get good results. These results often fade and the administrative departments never attempt any Lean activities. Lean gets written off as another "flavor of the month," another failed panacea. It's unfortunate because one would assume that as the factory processes become Lean, that it would then be obvious that the office processes supporting the factory—such as processing payroll, processing orders, paying bills, maintaining the facility, and managing engineering changes—also need to become Lean.

Organizations without manufacturing functions need a book geared to their requirements with tools and examples they can relate to. Organizations such as financial services and hospitals are notoriously inefficient and are more target rich than most factories.

The typical approach taken to improve the efficiency in an office is with automation. Unfortunately, this doesn't always work too well since automating a seriously flawed manual system is like paving the crooked cow path instead of constructing a straight new road.

In addition to discussing methods to assure that Lean initiatives don't fade, this book will discuss how Lean can be introduced to organizations where senior management has no interest in the subject and refuses to become involved.

Table of Contents

Sonic Industries Organization

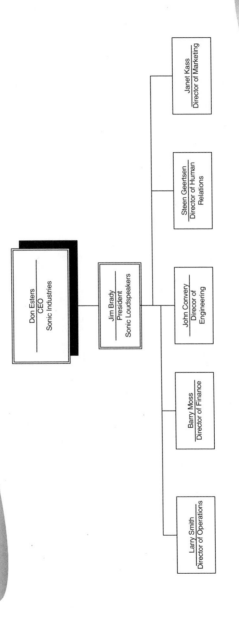

Don Esters
CEO
Sonic Industries

Jim Brady
President
Sonic Loudspeakers

Larry Smith
Director of Operations

Barry Moss
Director of Finance

John Convery
Direcor of
Engineering

Steen Geertsen
Director of Human
Relations

Janet Kass
Director of Marketing

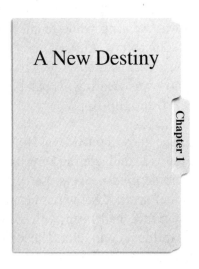

A New Destiny

Chapter 1

Larry Smith ended a grueling week at Sonic Labs. He got up Saturday morning, hoping to have a fun weekend and to put the week's stresses behind him. He poured himself a cup of coffee and walked to his family room window.

Across the street he saw Bob Simms, his friend and neighbor, scraping the price sticker from the window of a new, beautiful black sports car.

Both Larry and Bob had moved into the Royal Hills development five years earlier when the subdivision was first constructed. From day one, even though they were both about the same age, Bob Simms was always way ahead of Larry in terms of house upgrades, cars, and vacations.

Larry poured a second cup of coffee to bring to Bob, took both cups outside, and walked over to see the car. Larry was about to have a conversation that would change his destiny. "Hey Bob, nice car." Bob turned away from his scraping and smiled to see Larry. Bob was wearing white tennis shorts and a T-shirt with the words, "Innsbruck, Austria" above a skiing scene. This guy takes some great vacations, Larry thought, as he got closer to the car. Larry was wearing his paint-stained jeans, a torn and faded T-shirt, and flip-flops.

Larry and his wife, Sue, moved into Royal Hills five years ago when Larry took a job as Manufacturing Director at Sonic Labs, a manufacturer of home loudspeakers. Larry hadn't worked very long at Sonic before he discovered he was in over his head. His past experience had been with a manufacturing company that was a military contractor. The job was easy. The job at Sonic wasn't easy. Sonic was in a dog-eat-dog, highly competitive, consumer-product manufacturing business, and its problems were unlike anything Larry had experience in solving. To make things worse, Larry's boss, Jim Brady, was a bear to work for. Brady had a talent for demeaning and de-energizing people.

The friendship Larry developed with his neighbors, Bob and Lesley Simms, turned out to be fortuitous. The Simms moved to Royal Hills when Bob was recruited to become the Manufacturing Director of Apache, a domestic manufacturer of bicycle components. Bob was an expert in Lean Manufacturing and in a technique known as *Kaizen*. Bob was able to mentor Larry and teach him enough Lean techniques to not only keep him from getting fired but to turn a mess around.*

Larry went on to become Director of Operations. In the meantime, Bob's career took off. He was promoted to General Manager of Apache.

Bob put his hand on the roof of the car. "Larry, I finally got a Corvette. I've dreamed of owning a car like this since I was in high school. This has been a great year at Apache and I got a bonus check yesterday. I decided to buy myself a present." The sticker wasn't completely scraped off so Larry could see the price—$47,700.

Bob put the scraper down and accepted the coffee. "Thanks for the coffee, Larry. Let's sit down on my front steps. Tell me what's going on with you. We haven't had a talk in a while."

As they sat down, Larry looked out across the street to his own house. From where he was sitting, Larry could see Simms's magnificent lawn and ornamental shrubs, then the street and then his own brownish lawn, puny shrubs and five-year-old Ford Explorer in the driveway. The Simms's had opted for the largest model in the subdivision. The Smiths could only afford the least expensive one.

Larry wasn't envious of Bob's good fortune, but he did wish he knew as much about running a Lean business as Bob. "Well, Bob, you're right, we haven't spoken in a while. Thanks to your help, we turned manufacturing around and I was promoted from Director of Manufacturing to Director of Operations. I've

See the Discussion section at the end of this chapter for an explanation of Lean and Kaizen.

been very busy at work and putting in long hours, even on weekends."

Simms took a sip of coffee and offered, "Well I guess then that business is good?"

Larry paused to formulate a reply. "Since we implemented Lean in the factory, our customer service improved and our costs went down but there are still problems. Right after implementing Lean, our factory metrics improved dramatically. Output per person increased, scrap and rework dropped. But, I can't say we have *continuous improvement* at Sonic Labs.

"I think I'm the only manager at Sonic who has any interest in becoming Lean. The heads of the technical and administrative functions view Lean as strictly for the factory and want no part of it. We leaned out the factory but neglected to apply Lean to the functions that support the factory like processing orders, paying our bills, and managing engineering changes. My boss, Jim Brady, could care less. As a matter of fact, he's talking about outsourcing all of our manufacturing to China. He has been very upset with feedback from our customers who are complaining about our 70-day lead times. He's really on my case and has decreed that Sonic is losing money and being beaten up by our major customers for long lead times. He said that if we keep losing money at this rate, Sonic would go belly up. He told me yesterday that I'm supposed to get 20 percent of the cost out of the product and I have to go meet with our marketing department to develop a radically reduced lead time goal. He says that the reason he is seriously considering outsourcing our production to China is that supposedly, he can get our products made 20 percent lower there."

Bob got serious and began, "Larry your story is becoming more and more familiar. Lean gets implemented in operations, metrics improve dramatically for a while and then the metrics start to slip. In the meantime upper management has little or no interest in Lean and allows the people in engineering and administration to avoid any involvement in Lean initiatives.

"I know you have successfully improved performance in your machine shop and assembly operations. You can be very proud of that. But these improvements have not hit the financials in the same positive way. All you're doing is having isolated victories over waste without improving the performance of your whole enterprise. Unless Lean is applied to every function, starting with your suppliers and ending with delivery to your customer, you will not have a Lean Enterprise. A Lean *Enterprise* means a complete business system consisting of a product development process, a supplier management process, a fulfillment process from order through production to delivery, and a customer relations process through the useful lives of the products or services being provided. I'll email you a simple checklist* to see just how Lean your enterprise is."

"I'll take a look at the checklist but I think I already know that my company isn't Lean by any definition," replied Larry. "Three years ago when you spent one of your vacation weeks with me in my screwed-up factory you showed us how to apply Kaizen. You conducted a "Lean Kaizen Event" that reduced our internal lead time from three months to three days. And it only took five days with you, working with my team. The big lesson for us was that, to improve a process, you need to remove the waste. And you showed us how to discover the waste.

See Lean Enterprise Assessment Forms *in Appendix B.*

"The improvements we implemented stuck, but only manufacturing improved. Since then our overall lead time has increased and customers are starting to complain about late deliveries and short deliveries lately. The slippage of lead-times has nothing to do with my factory—it's the administrative function at Sonic that still has all the waste that needs to be removed. My boss is thinking of a radical downsizing of the company. He wants to keep marketing and product development here but leave only a miniscule manufacturing operation to build prototypes and our most expensive loudspeakers that are sold in very small volumes. He says that, even if our workforce worked for free, it would still be cheaper to get our products from China. He wants us to become nothing more than importers. If that happens I probably won't have a job.

"I'm getting bad vibes. I'm no longer invited to some meetings and haven't been cc'd on critical memos and e-mails.

"I don't want to play victim. I know there are lots of opportunities to improve operations but there's more to the company than operations. Operations is the easiest target to pick on. Our numbers are published daily for all to see. Anyone walking through the factory can easily spot waste. Anyone can look in the scrap bin and see what's being thrown out and anyone can spot workers in moments of idleness. I've read studies that show that 25 percent of the activities in a factory are wasteful. But 75 percent of the activities in a typical office are wasteful. The problem is that the waste in an office is hidden. It's hard to visualize the workflow in an office and, unlike factories, hardly any office measures its performance.

"You look into an office and see that most of the folks (if they are there) are working on their computers or involved in a meeting. They look busy, but are they doing work or playing on the Internet? They have in-baskets but who knows if the stuff there had been waiting for ten minutes or ten days? What is it waiting for anyway? How much of that stuff is causing my customers to get late deliveries?"

Simms was listening carefully to Larry rant and let his friend get it out of his system before commenting. "You are playing victim Larry. I will grant you that a lot of your troubles come from the administrative functions in your company. The problems show up in the factory but the root causes of the problems are often in the offices.

"The factory gets blamed for late deliveries, rising costs, and quality problem but these things can often be traced back to things like product development designing a product that can't be easily manufactured or is unreliable in field conditions, the sales department committing a schedule to the customer that the factory couldn't possibly deliver, ridiculous accounting rules, meaningless metrics, constantly changing plans, constantly changing priorities, improper selection of suppliers, insufficient liaison with customers, unnecessary meetings, and a zillion others. You can continue to play the role of the helpless victim and get steamrolled or you can once again do something about your situation."

Larry and Bob finished their coffee. Bob then said, "Larry come into the house and I'll get us another cup. I want to talk some more." As they entered the house, Bob's wife Lesley was walking across the living room on her way to the garage. "Hi guys," she sang and gave them both a big smile. "Haven't seen you in a while Larry. Sue says you've been working long hours."

"You're right, Lesley. My kids now call me 'Uncle Daddy.'"

Larry looked around at the Simms' house. What a terrific house, he thought as they made their way to the kitchen. Larry admired the beautiful custom furniture and great art on the walls. Larry and Sue had framed posters and a few numbered lithographs. The Simms had real art. Over the fireplace was an original oil painting of a sea battle between two sailing vessels shooting cannons at one another. Larry had seen paintings like this in museums but never in a private house. There was a Remington bronze statue of a cowboy on the coffee table. The Simms sure have trappings of success, thought Larry. Bob poured them two fresh cups of coffee that they took into Bob's office where they sat on his leather couch.

Bob then stood up, took a pad of paper from his desk, and walked across the room. He put the pad on his windowsill and then returned to his seat. "Larry, let me show you something. Let's say I have become very famous and let's say that I could sell a blank page with my signature on it for twenty-five dollars. Watch me as I make twenty-five dollars." Bob stood up, went to his desk drawer where he took out a pen, removed the cap from the pen, walked to the windowsill, tore off one piece of paper, walked back to his desk, sat down, signed his name to the paper, put the cap back on the pen, returned the pen to the drawer, walked to the windowsill where he placed the signed paper next to the pad, and then he sat back down.

"There, Larry, I just made twenty-five dollars. Watch me and I'll make another twenty-five dollars. I'll make a pile of signed papers and place them next to the pad for somebody to come get." Bob stood up again, walked to his desk drawer where he took out his pen, removed the cap, walked to the windowsill to take a page off the pad, walked back to his desk, sat down, signed his name, put the cap back on the pen, put the pen back in the drawer, walked to the windowsill where he placed the second signed paper on top of the first, and then walked back across the room to sit down.

"I just made fifty dollars, Larry. What do you think about that?" Larry was chuckling. "I don't think much of your process." "What's wrong with my process?" Bob asked. "I just made fifty dollars."

Larry replied, "You could make your process a lot simpler by just sitting at your desk with your uncapped pen in your hand, a pad on one side of you and an out basket on the other side."

Bob clapped his hands, "That's exactly right, Larry. My process was to take a worthless piece of paper and make it valuable by adding my signature to it. Signing my name *added value* to the paper. But the other activities you saw added no value. They were *non-value added activities*. Walking to the desk, getting the pen, uncapping and capping it, walking to the windowsill and back all added no value to the paper.

"And that's what happens in the office. Everyone is involved in doing work; everyone thinks they are working hard but not all the work adds value. The only work the customer will pay them to do is work that adds value.

"All you have to do is identify the non-value-added elements in your office processes and eliminate them. In my little signature illustration don't you think that 75 percent of my activities were waste?"

Larry thought for a few moments before answering. "That was a ridiculous illustration. My offices don't have that kind of wasted activity."

Bob quickly responded, "It's not a ridiculous illustration, I'll bet that you have just those kinds of non-value added activities going on, but you never took notice of them before."

Bob motioned his hand at Larry. "Come over here; I want to show you something." Bob took a fresh piece of paper from the pad and started to draw a simple sketch. "I want to show you a different way of looking at your costs at Sonic.

"The factory that you are responsible for produces a product; it's a physical product you can hold in your hand—a loudspeaker. People in Sonic's technical and administrative areas also produce a product, but it's not a technical product; it's a *knowledge product*. The knowledge products or the informational products are those that support your making of the physical product. Just like you have processes in the factory, the administrative and technical folks have their own processes. Their processes include things like creating the engineering drawings, creating the documentation, entering the customer orders, ordering raw materials, and paying the bills.

"Take a look at this sketch. The combined lengths of the two bars represent every bit of work that takes place in a typical company. The little bar represents only the value added work. Most people are surprised to learn that value added work represents only 0.5 to 5 percent of the total costs.

"You told me that your lead time is now seventy days. You leaned out the processes in fabrication and assembly and now only two of those days are in the factory. There's not much to be gained in the factory by improving value added time there. The low hanging fruit is in the remaining sixty-eight days in the administrative and technical areas.

"You have spent a lot of time gaining an understanding of everything that goes on in production but I don't think you know very much about the "products" that are produced in your office areas. Let's talk about where your company should focus their improvement efforts. Look at this sketch; the office areas are the least productive places in a company. That's where up to 99.5 percent of the non-value added work takes place.

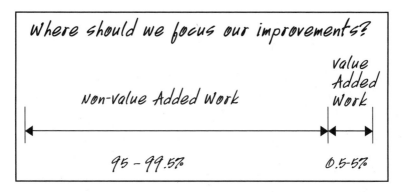

"What has to happen at Sonic is for the people in the administrative areas to focus on what the customer is willing to pay them to do and eliminate the work that doesn't add value. That's what's going to make those areas more efficient and reduce costs.

"And speaking of costs, I don't think your boss knows what he's talking about when he says that he can get the product 20 percent cheaper in China. He doesn't even know what the total cost of his product is now, nor does he understand the *total* costs associated with buying products from China. You need to convince Jim that he can cut 20 percent of his costs now and he doesn't have to outsource to China to do that.

"I can guarantee that if Sonic put their energies into reducing that 70-day lead time and reducing the non-value added work, your customers will appreciate it and your total costs will go down. Costs will go down because Lean companies do more and more with less and less. You will need fewer people in the administrative areas. You will be able to stop hiring additional administrative people and attrition will thin their ranks."

> *Some things have to be seen to be believed.*
> *But others have to be believed to be seen.*
>
> **Einstein**

Discussion

From a Lean management standpoint:
What's going on in this chapter?

Before taking his job at Sonic Labs, Larry had never heard of Lean. His neighbor Bob Simms introduced him to the concept.

The term "Lean" comes to us from Japan and was first described to Americans in a book published in 1990 called *The Machine That Changed the World*. This book by authors James Womack, Daniel Jones and Daniel Roos, describes Japanese management practices that enabled stunning success in the automotive and consumer electronics businesses.

When "Lean" companies are compared to ordinary companies, we see these differences:

√ Lean companies take one-half the human effort.

√ Lean companies have one-half the defects in the finished product or service.

√ Lean companies require one-third the engineering effort.

√ Lean companies use one-half the floor space for the same output.

√ Lean companies have 90% less inventory.

Companies who embark on the path to become Lean often do so because they have come to these conclusions:

- The business cannot continue operating the way it does—it won't survive.

- Everyone must change the way they do their jobs. Everyone!

The problem is knowing what to change and how to change. A useful technique for bringing about change very quickly is a *Kaizen*. Kaizen is a Japanese word meaning *continuous improvement* and is the most common technique employing the fundamental thinking for creating the Lean Enterprise. Kaizen involves studying the business process to discover where the waste is. Then a new process is implemented after all the waste has been removed.

Kaizen uses a technique called "the blitz" or "the event." An outside consultant, or better yet one of your own people, trained and experienced in the techniques can conduct the blitz. The strategy is to select one process in the company to improve. A blitz takes 3-5 days. A team of 6-12 people from across the organization is formed and given one full day of training in techniques to identify and eliminate waste. The focus of the team could be either a factory or an administrative function. The team then spends the rest of their time implementing the new, vastly improved process.

At the conclusion of the week, not only has a key business process been improved very quickly, but a team has been trained that can apply this same technique to other processes in the company. Unlike other improvement methods, Kaizen:

- Provides very quick implementation.

- Is low cost since it relies on your own people, not a gang of expensive consultants.

- Implants an effective team approach to problem solving and process improvement.

Three years ago Larry had his Kaizen Blitz and achieved stunning results in the factory. But his factory process improvements are eroding and the wastes in his company's administrative processes have not yet been uncovered.

Now let's return to Larry and Bob's conversation.

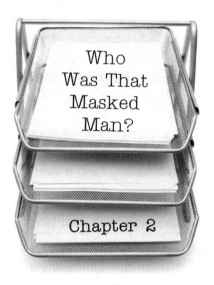

Who
Was That
Masked
Man?

Chapter 2

Larry tried to picture what went on in his offices. There were people constantly walking around. Fax machines and copiers were nowhere near the people who used them the most. In-baskets were usually pretty full, nothing could get done without approval signatures, and an incredible amount of time was spent in meetings. "Maybe Bob has a point," he thought.

"Okay Bob, maybe my administrative areas are full of waste. I don't know if I can do anything about it. My boss, Jim Brady, isn't interested in Lean," said Larry.

"Larry, I want to tell you a story. When I was a kid I used to watch the 'Lone Ranger' show on television and at the movie theater. Although the Lone Ranger was my favorite show, I realize now that the show's message poisoned our culture. I'll tell you what I mean by that.

"The show started out with this announcement: 'A fiery horse with the speed of light, a cloud of dust and hearty "Hi Ho Silver." With his faithful Indian companion, Tonto, the daring and resourceful masked rider of the plains led the fight for law and order in the early west. Return with us now to those thrilling days of yesteryear. The Lone Ranger rides again!'

"The Lone Ranger show was always about the same theme: helpless victims. Grandpa was living with his granddaughter and the rustlers were stealing their cattle. Or the widow was living with her son and the bank was going to foreclose on the mortgage and throw them out into the cold. Or perhaps Grandma was living with her grandson and the railroad company had decided to run the railroad tracks right through their living room. In every case these two people had something in common besides being helpless victims: they also happened to be the two stupidest people on the planet.

"The Lone Ranger and Tonto ride into town. The Lone Ranger, it is immediately apparent, has mystic qualities. He also has two pearl handled six shooters, a belt filled with silver bullets, and a magnificent super-horse named Silver.

"The Lone Ranger quickly sizes up the situation, outwits the culprits and rides off into the sunset singing 'Hi-Ho Silver, Away!'

"And as the Lone Ranger and Tonto ride off into the sunset with the town folks watching, somebody in the crowd asks,

'Who was that masked man?' And a chorus of voices reply, 'That was the Lone Ranger.' And off they disappear to the stirring strains of the William Tell overture.

"But what happens next? What happens is that new culprits come into town to cause new problems. The culprits are told by the town folks, 'You'll be very sorry you came to our town. We have the Lone Ranger.'

"Sorry folks, you don't have the Lone Ranger. The Lone Ranger is off helping other helpless victims. He isn't ever coming back to your town.

"Legends like 'The Lone Ranger' reinforce the message that we are all helpless victims and we can only be helped by heroes.

"Larry, are you waiting for the Lone Ranger? It sounds like you have two problems troubling you: manufacturing performance is declining, and you wish your boss would create a Lean Enterprise so that there was a focus on removing waste from the administrative functions in addition to the factory.

"I'll grant you that conventional wisdom holds that introducing Lean starts as a top-down program. It requires that the chief executive not only kicks off the effort but also is heavily involved with all aspects of the implementation. People in the middle layers of an organization, who find themselves working for a leader who has no interest in Lean, are often blinded by this paradigm and make little progress in reducing waste while waiting for the movement to start above them. These organizations can remain stagnant for long periods and may be left behind by their more nimble competition. Many people wonder what someone in the middle can do if he or she has a burning desire to implement Lean principles in the organization but knows that the superiors have little interest. After all, the superiors hold the purse strings and control the priorities. The common dilemma is how to kick off Lean throughout the enterprise, what tools to apply, how to design a comprehensive success plan, and how to do it without support from senior management.

"Larry, why don't you take a look at the survey document I emailed you and then we can talk about it. How about if we get together Sunday night?"

Larry could not enjoy the rest of his weekend. He took his two kids to a carnival on Saturday afternoon, went out to dinner and a movie that evening, and went fishing on Sunday. Then, just like every other Sunday around three o'clock in the afternoon, his mind was back at work. After dinner he downloaded Simms' survey document, read through it, and called Simms on the phone. "Bob, I just read your survey. I won't even bother to fill it out and get a score. I know my score would be lower than whale poop. Can I come over after dinner and talk to you about this?"

"Sure you can," Bob cheerfully responded. "I would love to help you."

After dinner Larry was sitting in Bob's den. Over Bob's desk was a photograph he was very proud of. It showed him standing next to a grinning Ronald Reagan.

"Larry, let me tell you about the classic implementation steps for Lean. These are the steps shown in most textbooks on the subject. Typically the first steps involve either the appointment of a change agent and perhaps some sort of organizational readiness assessment. Even before these steps take place, the senior executive must issue the 'call to action.' The entire organization must understand that the company can't keep up with demand or is in a crisis and that they will not survive unless they change the way they operate—and change very quickly. The call to action is vital in overcoming organizational inertia, flushing out cultural barriers to change, and in making it clear that the transformation must be enterprise-wide. *Everyone* must change."

Bob handed Larry a paper. "Here's a typical list of implementation steps."

Typical Steps to Implement Lean

1. Call to action
2. Business assessment
3. Get training and/or a *sensei*
4. Create a Lean Promotion function (an implementation officer and a team)
5. Map the Value Streams to develop current and future states
6. Begin Kaizen Events
7. Implement new metrics to assure that people will be held accountable for performance
8. Expand Lean disciplines throughout the enterprise and to suppliers

Clearly, your implementation would be very non-conventional since it would be accomplished with only passive upper management support, at least at first. We should consider a different approach. Although it is often possible to start a corporate-wide effort, it takes much more effort to keep it going than it does to derail it. This is especially true in companies that are doing well, growing, and generally not in a corporate-wide crisis. Even if you were able to get a top-down initiative started, I have a feeling that the next 'fire' or crisis would distract the key participants.

"The problem with the traditional model is that nothing much really happens visibly until Step 6— the Kaizen Events. During all the steps leading up to that point, there's a lot of activity, but not much visible improvement in the organization. The effort is easily resource constrained, ignored and ultimately crushed.

"The alternative is a radical paradigm jump—simply start the process at Step 6—the Kaizen Blitz, also called the Lean Event or Breakthrough Project. Use a quick, big victory to give the company an insatiable addiction to Lean by giving it a good dose of the benefits up front. That's exactly what we did for you and your team in your factory but Lean didn't spread to any administrative functions. This time you should do a Lean Event in an administrative area. Are any of your peers interested in Lean?"

Larry pondered the question for a moment. "Steen Geertsen is the Director of HR. He's my buddy and has read books on Lean. He has always supported the shop floor activities. I think he would be very interested in joining me in spreading Lean throughout the organization and in learning how to use Lean principles to identify and remove waste from administrative processes."

> *Tell me I'll forget.*
> *Show me I may remember.*
> *Involve me and I'll understand.*
>
> **Chinese Saying**

Discussion

From a Lean management standpoint:
What's going on in this chapter?

Bob asks Larry if he was waiting for the Lone Ranger—the mythical hero. In our culture we place a tremendous reliance not only on *heroes* but also on *stars*.

We treat the fireman as a hero because he can put out the fire. But we don't treat the plant manager who never had a fire as a hero.

The heroes and stars in our organization can put out our fires. They solve our problems when they pop up because they thoroughly understand our systems and know how to get around the systems. If our heroes and stars left, we wouldn't know how to function.

Heavy reliance on heroes and stars isn't a problem. It's a symptom of a problem and that problem is a lack of standardization. There is very little reliance on heroes and stars in companies where their key processes have become *standardized.*

Chapter 3

The
Conspiracy

Larry woke up Monday morning eager to get to work and to try to get his friend Steen—Sonic's HR Director—involved with an enterprise-wide Lean initiative.

"Larry, you're nuts!" was the first comment from Steen after hearing his proposal. "First of all, we're going to get zero support from our dear boss, Jim Brady, and second of all, I can't believe that finance, engineering, or marketing will have any interest at all." Larry and Steen were sitting in Steen's office. Fifteen years ago, Steen moved to America from Denmark where he was educated and where he played semi-pro soccer. He was a "big boy." On the wall of his office was a framed poster of Copenhagen.

"Listen, Steen, I implemented Lean principles in the factory and got almost miraculous results. I cut my lead times from three months to three days. My friends in the technical and administrative areas were impressed but they didn't see how Lean could help them. They thought Lean was strictly a 'factory thing.'

"Let me tell you about that factory thing. Things were terrible in the factory when I started here as production manager. I thought I was going to get fired. All I got from Brady was threats, and the only advice he offered was to exhort the people in the factory to work as hard as they could. Effective leaders know that dramatic improvement can't be made by exhortation. It takes a lot more than inspirational speeches, incentives or threats. The change has to come from process improvements. The only way I know to get Brady his 20 percent cost reduction and reduce our lead times is to implement Lean throughout this company.

"The problem is what to change and how to change. You may remember that the method we used to kick things off was to bring in an outsider who wouldn't miss the forest for the trees. My friend and neighbor, Bob Simms, told me about a technique called Kaizen that brings about change very quickly. Kaizen is a Japanese word meaning *continuous improvement* and the Kaizen Event is the most common tool for creating the Lean Enterprise. He taught me that application of Kaizen involves a study of the business's processes in an effort to discover where the waste is. Then a new process is implemented after much, if not all, the waste has been removed.

"The amazing thing about Kaizen is the speed of implementation. I knew that there were many consulting companies who pour expensive teams into the client's company and spend months gathering data. This data gathering often just culminates in a three-ring binder chocked full of terrific ideas. The binder often resides on the boss's desk and the terrific ideas never get implemented.

"At my level I couldn't hire a consultant and I needed improvement quickly. Bob Simms generously offered to spend a week here in our factory doing Kaizen.

"At the conclusion of our week doing Kaizen, not only did our fabrication and assembly departments improve very quickly, but also a team had been trained to apply this same technique to other processes in the factory. Unlike other improvement methods, Kaizen provides very quick implementation, is low cost since it relies on your own people instead of expensive, entry-level consultants, and implants an effective team approach to problem solving and process improvement.

"I'll admit that my Lean program in the factory has slipped a bit but if we could make Lean an enterprise-wide effort, we could have a sustainable turnaround at Sonic. I thought that after Brady saw how much improvement we got in the factory by applying Lean principals he would want to apply those principles to the processes that support the factory. It never happened. I can tell you a few administrative processes that can use a Lean approach. Customers who call customer service are left on hold for ten minutes, our delivery of spare parts is often incomplete and usually late, our delivery times are slipping, and it's taking longer and longer to introduce new models.

"If we could have a Lean event in an administrative area that produced dramatic results we could get our peers interested in Lean even if Brady isn't interested. What I learned from Bob Simms was that there are three requirements to be met when selecting a process to improve. First, the customer has to benefit from the improvement. Second, the process has to be dysfunctional. And third, it should have a high likelihood of success. Is there a process in HR that satisfies those requirements, Steen?"

Steen looked up at the ceiling as if the answer to Larry's question would be printed there. "I can think of one process I would like to improve but you may think it's trivial. Were you thinking that we tackle a project such as reducing the new product introduction cycle or decreasing the days to do the month-end financial close? Because I don't have anything like that in my little personnel department."

"No, Steen, I don't think we should tackle anything that big at first. That would be like boiling the ocean as far as I'm concerned. I think we should pick a simple project that has a high likelihood of success but one that will let us use as many Lean tools as possible during a Kaizen event. What project did you have in mind?"

"I'm almost embarrassed to tell you what I have in mind, you may find it so trivial. As you know, even though business is soft, this is a seasonal business and we've been hiring quite a few people. The new hires are given a 'new hire package.' It's a two-inch thick packet of papers and pamphlets dealing with benefits and company policies. I was watching the clerk assemble a package for a new employee and I couldn't believe how long it was taking her. There must be a lot of waste in that process.

"But Larry, I don't think we can just pick a process to improve and form a team to fix it. I've been reading about Lean on the internet and all the experts say you need to start off with a training program. Shouldn't we train all our personnel before we tackle any process improvements? I received a brochure from a company that offers a ten-week Lean training program for a reasonable fee. They call their program Soft Skills Lean Training. They cover things like conflict resolution, reaching consensus, leading change, managing diversity, goal setting, team problem solving, group facilitation, listening skills, team formation, how to run an effective meeting, and presentation skills."

Larry had been standing in front of the Copenhagen poster looking at the artist's depictions of the neighborhoods. He turned around to face Steen. "Steen, I know a lot of Lean efforts begin with soft-skill training, but I can tell you what argues against it. First, this training often has a stale, canned feel to it —everyone who has been through training on these topics has had more than they can stomach. And if you tell people they are going through them again, you're gonna get disinterest or half-hearted support at best.

"Second, the training requires resources and time from the team. They are often already very busy, so the senior management who see little reward resents it. Finally, the training imposes a time-delay between the beginning of the effort and the first payoff. This time-delay is time in which things can go wrong; a critical player can leave the company, an unrelated crisis can pop up. This is time where little good occurs and a lot of things can go wrong.

"This is not to say that training is not important—it's vital to the effort. But it needs to accomplish a critical thing beyond the transfer of knowledge—it needs to light fire in the bellies of the players. In some respects, the training is like the locker-room pep talk before the big game. Part of the goal is to leave the team red-hot for action. Training that takes a few weeks or is spread out over time just cannot do this. The training has to be done fast—one day tops—and then put to use immediately.

"There's a theory about training. If you train people in a skill and they don't get to apply the training within two days, that training is wasted. There was no way I would get support for a 10-week training course on soft-skills. The people involved would not support it, and, more important, their bosses would not support it. When Bob Simms conducts a Lean event, he incorporates the critical training into the first day of a one-week event. Not much can go wrong in just one day. And, if the weeklong event is successful, it will catalyze a chain-reaction that results in a huge, demonstrable improvement in just one week.

"There's another reason I don't like long training programs as a way to kick off Lean. Let's say I somehow get Brady to agree to implement Lean on an enterprise-wide basis. I convince him to let me have $30,000 as a budget. I then kick off the program with ten weeks of training. At the end of the first month he sees no progress in his company. Deliveries and costs are still the same. At the end of two months he still sees no improvement. At the end of ten weeks he has spent $30,000 and nothing has improved except some folks attended a class. But if we go ahead and do some Lean events, by the end of ten weeks, there will have been major improvements in the company.

"Three years ago when Bob Simms conducted a Kaizen Event here in manufacturing, the event took one week. The first day was devoted to training on Lean principles and Kaizen techniques. By the end of the week we had implemented major improvements in the fabrication and assembly areas. The Kaizen Blitz was perfect for our needs. Back then I thought a big part of what was needed in manufacturing was training. Bob Simms designed the Kaizen Blitz so that all the training happened on day one, without dragging out the process and allowing it to lose momentum. He taught me that if I could get just a few people excited about Lean, I could start a fire that could not be extinguished.

"And that's what happened. Our initial improvements were dramatic and we got even better as time went on and we continually improved. But nothing like that happened in the administrative areas. Brady is disgusted with the complaints he's getting from our customers about our long lead times. He's thinks that the only salvation for Sonic is to go the outsourcing route.

"Now I want to start a new Lean program but this time do it enterprise-wide. Using the first day of the Blitz for training is essential. We could invite our senior management to the training, and they could get some first-hand exposure to Lean without starting a big program or making a big investment.

"I would love to kick this off with Brady leading the charge. In an ideal world the senior executive would issue the 'call to action.' The entire organization must understand that the company can't keep up with demand or is in a crisis, and that they will not survive unless they change the way they operate— and change very quickly. The call to action is vital in

31

overcoming organizational inertia, flushing out cultural barriers to change and in making it clear that the transformation must be enterprise-wide. Everyone must change.

"In our case this implementation will have to be different since we can't count on active support from Brady, at least at first.

"Here's what I think we should do. Why don't we plan a Kaizen event? Since your 'new hire package' project isn't very complex, we could do a three-day event. The first day would be devoted to training and the next two would be in improving the process. We could form a small team to spend the three days on the project—maybe use the three folks from HR and then get three more people from engineering, finance, and marketing. But I would love to invite ten people to the first day so that we train a cross section of technical and administrative people in the fundamentals of Lean Administration.

"I need to go start my day now. It's almost time to kick off my daily staff meeting. I'm going to talk to the heads of engineering, marketing, and finance and try to convince them to sit in on the first day of training."

Just then Jim Brady walked into Hans' office. "Good morning guys. How are my favorite operations and HR leaders doing? What are you two discussing so seriously?"

Steen was quick to reply. "Good morning Jim, we were just talking about last night's game. What have you been up to?"

"I'm going to make your lives a lot more pleasant gentlemen. As you know I've been talking to a Chinese company about moving our manufacturing to China. The initial quotes are almost unbelievable. They can deliver our product here from

China for less than we now pay just for materials. I can cut 75 percent of the personnel from this operation. I'm planning to spend most of today with an Asian outsourcing consultant."

> *The doctors told me I would never walk again,*
> *but my mother told me I would,*
> *so I believed my mother.*
>
> **Wilma Rudolf**
> **(Winner of 3 Gold Metals, 1960 Olympics)**

Discussion

From a Lean management standpoint:
What's going on in this chapter?

Larry's company introduced Lean into the factory but it never spread beyond the factory into the administrative and technical areas. Some people argue that starting Lean in the administration and technical areas can be a more effective way to transform an organization than starting at the end of the process (as in the cases where the company does manufacturing).

While that may work with certain companies, it is a risky approach for two reasons. The first reason is that Kaizen events in factories produce almost instantaneous dramatic results. The enthusiasm created by the success is often infectious and spreads quickly to the rest of the organization. Since most office processes are typically much more waste-laden than manufacturing processes, Kaizen events there produce even more dramatic savings but, unlike a factory, the savings are not instantaneously realized. Administrative improvements often require computer programming changes or organizational restructuring that could take weeks or months of implementation. The enterprise-wide implementation, therefore, could be slow or stall completely. Starting Lean in the factory creates excitement and a high degree of momentum that drives the program forward.

The second argument for starting improvements at the end of the process is that the end of the process is closest to the customer and therefore benefits the customer.

Chapter 4

Chinese Postmortem

After dinner Larry saw Bob practicing casts with a fly rod on his front lawn. He walked across the street and was greeted by Bob. "Hey Larry, look at this cool fly-fishing outfit I just got on Ebay. How's the loudspeaker business?"

"I'm really upset, Bob. It looks like my boss is getting serious about building our products offshore. He says he can get our product made in China and shipped here for less than we currently pay for materials."

Bob put the fly rod down on the lawn. "It's funny you're mentioning that this evening because I had a phone call today from a buddy, Paul Johnson, who told me a story about a catastrophe his company had with a Chinese supplier.

"Paul was in charge of operations for a company in Los Angeles that made expensive skateboards. They were manufacturing their most popular board for $47. That broke down to $28 for materials, $4 for labor, and $15 for overhead. The owner of the company received a quote from a factory in mainland China who said they could deliver the skateboard to Los Angeles for $19. That's even less than they were paying for material alone. The Chinese company was ISO-certified and had a list of American companies they were already making skateboards for. It seemed too good to be true. How could they resist?

"So they contracted with the company in China and initially things were going well. Deliveries were on time and the quality seemed okay. The only thing they didn't consider was all the time they would have to spend traveling to China. To get things started, they had to send a manufacturing engineer and a quality guy to China for a few weeks. They assumed that they would only have to send somebody there about twice a year after the initial setup.

"A few months later the problems started. Paul's incoming inspection department in California found defects in the Chinese skateboards. Luckily none of the defective boards were shipped to customers. They sent a quality engineer to China who had to spend three weeks there. Defects in their material were causing the defective finished skateboards. The engineer discovered that the Chinese company had discontinued their incoming inspection because their raw material was coming from a sister plant that they trusted. The Chinese very reluctantly agreed to re-institute incoming inspection. By the time the source of the problem was discovered, and the inventory of defective material was sorted, the only way to maintain their schedule was to make the next shipment by air.

"Paul decided to hire his own Chinese inspector to oversee quality in his supplier's plant. He ultimately found out that this inspector was totally intimidated by plant management and became useless.

"The next problem was late deliveries. The factory in China was having problems with employee turnover—not just production workers, but engineers and administrative personnel as well. This is a serious problem in China now. People are quitting their jobs to get a few dollars more at the factory across the street.

"At that point the company thought about moving some of the production back to the U.S. but that wasn't possible. To get the Chinese operation going they had moved their assembly line from America to the Chinese plant. They figured it would take six months to replace it and re-staff the operation in the states. They couldn't afford to take six months to solve the problem with the China production.

"Paul had to send two production engineers to China for a month to keep production going. During their two-year experience with the Chinese supplier, these problems with late deliveries, airfreight, and sending personnel to China persisted. There were typically five people a month getting sent to China to resolve production or quality problems. Quality engineers, design engineers and manufacturing engineers were routinely visiting the China operation. These trips cost an average of $3,000 each. The costs were adding up. The company initially thought they would be getting the skateboard for $19 but when they added up the excess freight charges and the trips to China, they found the true cost was closer to $30, still a lot better than the $47 they were paying to build it themselves. The difference was worth the headaches. Or so they thought.

"Without realizing it, with all those key personnel out of the American plant, they began falling behind on their new product introductions. They thought about adding additional personnel, but there was no way they could get new hires up to speed on the projects in time. And if they did add more personnel, their profits would have eroded even further.

"Then to compound the situation, their main competitors (who had decided not to move operations to China) released a new technology they were also trying to develop and seized a large part of their market share. The distraction of the problems in China robbed them of the critical resources they needed to develop new products.

"Then the real problem hit. There were three field failures resulting in injuries due to defective die-castings. That caused two problems, the least of which was the cost to settle the personal injury claims. Once word got out about the problems, orders stared to slip. Sales got worse and worse. And today I got a call from Paul to tell me his company is now bankrupt.

"I'm not saying it's a mistake to move production from America to China. What I am saying is that 'things aren't always as they seem'. Just because the company claims to be ISO-certified, has a list of impressive customers and has a slick brochure doesn't mean they're okay. Outsourcing may look like a good move for some companies, but doing business with a manufacturer a few thousand miles away, shipping components on huge slow-moving cargo ships, dealing with language barriers leading to miscommunications, and just avoiding a swindle isn't as simple as it may look.

"This year we heard about the product recalls in America because of serious quality problems with Chinese suppliers of such things as dog food, toothpaste, computer batteries, and toys. You can be certain that these Chinese suppliers were carefully chosen, were probably ISO-certified, and that the tremendous costs associated with the recalls were not anticipated in the justification to get Chinese suppliers in the first place.

"When making such decisions, it's not simply a matter of comparing our in-house costs to the quote from China. Total Supplier Cost must be considered."

Simms walked over to his bookshelf and pulled down a booklet and opened it to a page to show Larry. "I got this handout at a seminar I attended on Total Supplier Costs. This page has a list of metrics to be considered when calculating the total cost of a supplier."

Some Metrics of Total Supplier Costs

- Quality level
- Service level
- Correct quantity
- On-time delivery
- Ramp up and ramp down ability
- Price/cost of product
- Use of electronic data interchange
- Willingness to share sensitive information
- Presence of certification or other documentation
- Flexibility to respond to unexpected demand changes
- Communication skills/systems (phone, fax, e-mail, Internet)
- Quick response time in case of emergency, problem, or special request
- Willingness to change their products and services to meet your changing needs
- Willingness to participate in your firm's new product development and value analysis
- Currency stability

"Things like those on the list aren't always considered when selecting a supplier. Another major consideration aside from quality costs is the "relationship costs." Those include costs like my skateboard maker incurred by having all those people taking unexpected trips to Asia. Let me give you an idea of some of the costs, aside from just the quote, that need to be considered when using the Total Supplier Cost concept.

"There's something called Flexibilty or Customization Costs. Very often the supplier will charge an outrageous upcharge for a simple modificaton you need to make to the original design. The supplier knows he has you as a captive customer and can take advantage of the situation. That's not considered when comparing your in-house quote to the the one from abroad.

"The transit time from Asia is also an important consideration. This often demands that you keep extra safety stock, and that is also an added and often overlooked cost.

"Two important considerations are your supplier's ability to respond to demand fluctuations and your product's end of life costs. Suppliers can have very impressive abilities to respond to the initial orders. But once they get rolling, it may be difficult for them to ramp up or ramp down from an ongoing output level. This could result in serious shortages or bloated inventories. There is also the danger of a major write off which often happens at the end of a product's life if the supplier can't be shut off quickly.

"I think Jim Brady has to be very careful when he compares the China quotes to your in-house cost of manufacturing. I'm sure you will get a very impressive quote from potential China sources. But you can be sure that the quote will not include any of the types of costs listed on this pamphlet page.

"You need to compare the total supplier costs to your in-house costs. Brady thinks he can save 20 percent. But remember, your current in-house costs reflect the wasteful way your company is run today. The question is, 'What would your in-house costs be if you were able to take the waste out of your administrative systems?' Another interesting question is, 'How much better would customer service be if the waste were removed from your administrative systems?' We are in a world where prompt and speedy delivery is as important as price.

"Yesterday I went to have my oil changed at a place that advertised 'Ten Minute Oil Change.' And they really did change my oil in ten minutes. Actually it was eight and one-half minutes. I would have been impressed, except that I had to wait in line for forty minutes before the oil change started.

"I think you're suffering from the same problem. You carefully measure the time it takes for your product to get from incoming raw material through to shipment to the customer. That's a fine metric to track for your factory, but just like the ten-minute oil change, the metric doesn't reflect the customer's experience. The customer is interested in how long it takes from the time he places his order until he receives the part.

"I've been through your offices and, believe me, it's what I call a 'Target-Rich Environment' for waste removal.

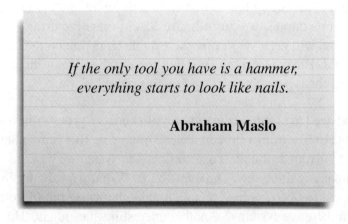

If the only tool you have is a hammer,
everything starts to look like nails.

Abraham Maslo

Chapter 5

Planning for Kaizen

Larry Smith and Steen Geertsen invited John Convery, head of the engineering department, and Barry Moss, head of finance to lunch to try to convince them to participate in a Kaizen event in the personnel department. Neither was enthusiastic.

John Convery explained, "I've read about Lean and I think it's a terrific thing for removing waste from the factory floor. I'm sorry to tell you, Larry, but I think there's still a lot of low hanging fruit on your factory floor that hasn't been picked. I don't see why my engineers have to be involved with Lean. You've got to understand, we're 'inventors' and you can't constrain us by treating the design process as just another link in the factory's chain."

Barry Moss interjected, "I feel the same way about my finance operation. My office isn't like a factory where hourly workers process parts on conveyor belts or inside machinery. Computers process our work. Your factory improvement tools can't possibly work in an office environment."

Larry knew he had to be diplomatic and persuasive if he wanted to enlist John and Barry's support. "John, I have tremendous respect for your engineers. I think they're geniuses and without them we wouldn't have any products. But you must know that studies have shown that more than 70 percent of a product's cost, quality, and customer value are influenced at the design stage. Everyone knows that Toyota invented the Lean tools that made their factories so efficient. But these same types of Lean tools at Toyota's engineering departments helped make them the consistently most profitable carmaker who never missed major milestones, developed products 50 percent faster than its competitors, and had the highest quality in the automotive industry."

At that point, Steen pointed at Barry Moss and began, "Barry, you and I both run office operations. We both wish we could be more efficient. You are frustrated with how long it takes you to do the month-end close. I'm frustrated with my leave-of-absence process."

He then pointed at John. "Engineering has their own dysfunctional processes. It takes you guys weeks to process the simplest design change request. We can all stand to remove waste from our operations. I'm volunteering to use my department to conduct a pilot administrative Kaizen event. Larry has had experience with his factory Kaizen events so he's going to lead mine. We've picked a very simple process to improve—the preparation of new-hire paperwork.

"We want to form a cross-functional team to work for three days to learn Kaizen tools to improve this process. Then this team can return to their own departments to apply these tools to improve more complex processes there.

"If Brady follows through with his plans to outsource to China, neither of us will have any department to manage. The best shot we have is to dramatically improve our processes here at Sonic. I think Lean tools can be applied to service, technical, and administrative processes. What do we have to lose?"

By the time they all finished lunch, Barry and John had reluctantly agreed to let Larry conduct a Kaizen event in the Human Resources department. They would attend along with one other member from their departments.

> *Feelings of worth can flourish only in an atmosphere where individual differences are appreciated, mistakes are tolerated, communication is open, and rules are flexible - the kind of atmosphere that is found in a nurturing family.*
>
> **Virginia Satir**

Chapter 6

Kaizen in the
HR Department

A team of ten was formed. Steen Geertsen had his HR supervisor and two clerks join the team. Barry Moss of finance had his cost accountant, John Convery had his assistant, and the marketing department had two people from customer service.

The team met in the HR conference room on Monday morning. Larry explained that they would spend the next three days together conducting a Kaizen Blitz, also known as a Kaizen Event. He explained that Kaizen is a Japanese term meaning *continuous improvement* and although it's usually thought of as a method to improve factory operations, it is even more effective in service and administrative applications.

Larry drew the "Focus on improvement" illustration that Bob Simms showed him and explained how little of the work that takes place in offices adds value.

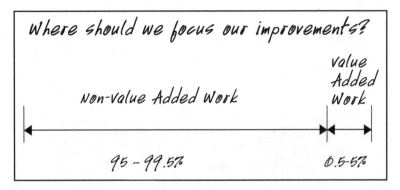

He made it clear that the three days would require a full-time effort. That meant the team would stay together; nobody would return to their departments to attend meetings or to check messages. The objective of the three-day event was to reduce by 50 percent the time it took Patty in the Human Resources department to assemble the paperwork given to all new employees. The package of papers was referred to as the "start pack."

The team was shocked by the goal. A 50 percent improvement seemed like a ridiculous challenge. 10 percent would be more realistic to achieve in just a few days.

Larry spent an hour explaining the philosophy of Kaizen and handed out a sheet with an explanation of terms*. The key point Larry made was that, in order to get better results, you need to improve the process. The way to improve a process is to discover the waste in the process and permanently remove

*See explanation of Kaizen terms in appendix

it. Although that sounds simple enough, the problem is that the waste in the process, the activities that add no value, are usually well hidden. The waste in a factory is simpler to find since the workflow is easy to visualize and factories usually abound with metrics (although many are misleading at their best and often incorrect at their worst). Office workflow is very difficult to visualize and there are typically few metrics. The Kaizen methodology provides a structured approach to discovering office waste.

Larry explained that they picked a very simple project that would give team members an opportunity to learn some fundamental Kaizen tools that they could then take to their own areas to improve the more complex processes there.

The team was provided with juice, coffee, and doughnuts at the start of the meeting. When Larry finished his explanation of Kaizen fundamentals he said, "I'm now going to give each of you a stack of red tags. When you're through with your coffee I want you, as a team, to go out to the Human Resource office area and put a red tag on anything that you think won't be used in the next thirty days. You have exactly twenty minutes to complete that. When you're through, Steen will look at what you've tagged and if the stuff really won't be used in the next thirty days he will arrange to either throw it away or move it to a remote location called a 'Red Tag Area.'"

Patty, the clerk from HR spoke up, "That's ridiculous! We need everything in our department. If it wasn't needed we would have gotten rid of it before this."

"I'm not too sure of that, Patty," Larry responded. "I took a walk through your department this morning and saw a carton filled with invitations to the company picnic that was held five years ago. Just give this process a chance and take twenty minutes to do the red tag campaign."

The groups descended on the HR office. Twenty minutes later, they were amazed at how many items they found that would not be used in the next thirty days.

Results of Red Tag Campaign

After the team reassembled in the HR conference room, Larry explained, "There are a few reasons I wanted to kick off this three-day event with a Red Tag exercise. First of all, I wanted to get the clutter out of the area before we begin serious observations and measurements. And secondly, I wanted to show you how, by working together in a structured fashion, we could accomplish a great deal in a very short period of time. We have to learn to see the waste before we can actually remove it."

Larry continued, "The next thing I want us to do is actually study the process Patty goes through in assembling the Start Pack. I want two of you to take a stopwatch and time everything Patty does from start to finish. In addition to measuring how long the process takes, I want to know how long each element of the process takes. I'll give you a stopwatch to use.

"At the same time, I want one of you to draw a 'spaghetti diagram' also known as a 'dance chart.' It's a simple sketch of the path Patty takes while assembling the pack. While the three of you are capturing the times and drawing the dance chart, the rest of you carefully observe what Patty does."

Time Study - 30 second tick mark increments (based on cycle time)							
				WASTE			
Station or Operation #: Assemble Employee Start Pack	Value Add (Copy & Assemble)	Wait	Search	Walking	Correct/Rework	Other	TOTAL "tick marks" & total time
Study #1	IIIIIIIIII IIIIIIIIIII IIIIIIIII		IIII	IIIIIIIIIII IIIIIII			55
Time	16'		2'	9'30"			27'30"
#2	IIIIIIIIIII IIIIIIIIIII IIIIIIIII		III	IIIIIIIIIII IIIIIIIII			54
Time	15'30"		1'30"	10'			27'
#3	IIIIIIIIIII IIIIIIIIIII IIIIIIII		III	IIIIIIIIIII IIII		I	49
Time	15'		1'30"	7'30"		30"	24'30"
#4	IIIIIIIIIII IIIIIIIIIII IIIIIIIIII		IIIII	IIIIIIIIIII IIIIIII			56
Time	16'		2'30"	9'30"			28'
#5	IIIIIIIIIII IIIIIIIIIII IIIIIIIII		IIII	IIIIIIIIIII IIIIII		I	54
Time	16'		2"	8'30"		30"	27'

Waste Elimination Time and Motion Study

Steps to Assemble Employee Start Pack	Minutes
Walking	9
Searching	2
Assembling	12
Copying	4
Total	**27**

The Time Study

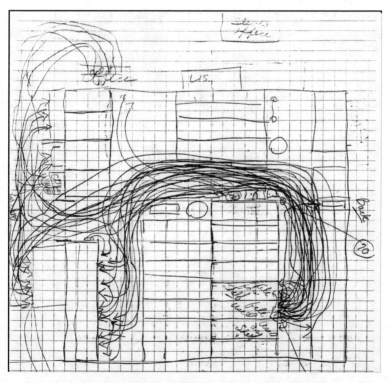

The Spaghetti Diagram Before Kaizen, 2442 Feet of Walking to Assemble One Pack

The team reassembled in the conference room after about half an hour. Larry began, "There's a Japanese expression, 'Speak with Data.' Now we have data to help us to begin to understand our process. We know that the process takes Patty twenty-seven minutes to complete. Patty, did you know you walked over twenty-four hundred feet to complete a Start Pack?"

Patty's mouth dropped, "I can't believe I walk almost half a mile every time I assemble a pack. I've been going to the gym after work every day to use the treadmill. I didn't realize I was already getting my daily workout on the job."

Larry tacked the time study and spaghetti chart on the wall. "This is a good start to understanding our process. The next step is the most important. It's called the MUDA hunt. Taiichi Ohno, while developing the Toyota Production System, came up with what he called the Seven Deadly Wastes called MUDA in Japanese. Waste is endemic to all processes in all organizations. As I've told you, 95 percent of all activities that make up the time to produce and deliver a product to the customer are non-value added and can be eliminated or minimized using Lean concepts. A MUDA hunt is a structured approach for a team to use to discover the elements in a process that add no value. If the team just wandered into the HR department and looked for waste as best they can, they would have a tough time. That's because the processes you see every day look 'normal' to you. That's the way you always see the process. The MUDA hunt will give you 'new eyes' with which to look at your process.

"We all know that the customer pays only for our value added activities. There are only two types of activities that take place during a process: the value added (VA) and the non-value added

(NVA). We have to find the non-value added." He listed Toyota's seven categories of MUDA on a flipchart and taped the paper to the wall with the other papers.

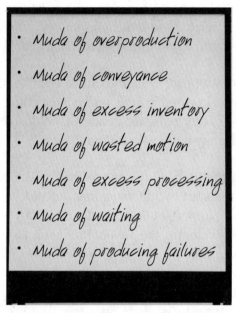

- Muda of overproduction
- Muda of conveyance
- Muda of excess inventory
- Muda of wasted motion
- Muda of excess processing
- Muda of waiting
- Muda of producing failures

Larry explained the definition of each form of waste. He then split the group into two teams and told them they had twenty minutes to make a list of the different types of MUDA Patty performed while doing her Start Pack process. He had a preprinted form defining each form of MUDA with a space below for writing in what the team discovered.

"When you fill out these forms, I would like you to list your observations in the form of questions—not in the form of accusations. We are questioning the process, not Patty's efforts. We have enough fear and judgementalism in this organization. So write each observation in the form of a *Why* question."

Larry's pre-printed MUDA HUNT form:

Muda Hunt

7 Types of Waste in Service and Administrative Areas

1. **Overproduction**: Producing more than is needed or before it is needed. Too many people delivering services. Supplying more information than needed. Producing work for which there are no orders. Creating reports nobody reads. Making extra copies.

2. **Inventory**: Maintaining excess inventory of raw material, work in progress or finished goods causing longer lead times, obsolete or damaged goods, storage costs and delays. Files waiting to be worked on. Open projects. Emails waiting to be read. Too many forms, office supplies, computers. Unused records in a database.

3. **Transportation**: Wasted effort to transport paperwork into and out of storage or between processes. Going to get signatures.

4. **Waiting**: Any non-value added time. Waiting for meetings to begin. Papers waiting in an in-box for someone else's input. Having no work because of stock outs or capacity bottlenecks. Waiting for faxes. Waiting for the system to come back up. Waiting for customer response. Waiting for a handed off file to come back.

5. **Motion:** Any wasted motion like walking to get information or paperwork. Searching for a form or office supply. Extra clicks or keystrokes. Clearing away files on a desk. Gathering information. Looking through manuals and catalogs. Handling paperwork.

6. **Over-processing**: Providing higher quality than is necessary. Extra operations such as producing a 15-page report when one page will do. Taking unneeded steps to process the work. Repeated entry of data.

7. **Correction**: Audits, checking. Decisions made at a meeting and then re-made. Pricing error. Missing information. Lost records.

After twenty minutes, the teams returned to the conference room, consolidated their observations onto one set of flip chart pages, and pasted them onto the wall.

Muda Hunt Results

Muda of Overproduction

- Why are 5 copies made at a time whether they are needed or not?

- Why are there so many forms? Are they all required?

Muda of Inventory

- Why are there too many of some things (i.e., provider directories) and not enough inventory of other things (i.e., Credit Union Brochures, Xerox copies of some forms)?

- Why is there not an inventory control system in place?

- When making copies, why not check all forms to see if other copies are needed and do them all at once?

Transportation:

- Why the unnecessary trips to the copier to make forms when there should always be a supply in the folder?

- Why are there so many trips from the file cabinets to the outer table to the bookshelves to the file cabinets?

- Why isn't everything all in one place?

- Why are the forms not in the order of use?

- Why are there no stapler, scissors, tape, and hole punch close by the work area or the copy machine?

- Why are the items not pulled in order? (Alphabetical or the order of the sheet)?

- Why don't the medical-related forms go into one section?

- Why are the books in different places?

- When working on books, why replenish shelves at the same time . . . why not finish the packages then go back and replenish shelves for next time?

Muda of Waiting

- Why do the phones have to be answered and interruptions made to the person who is compiling the packages?

Muda of Motion

- Why do there have to be trips to the copy machine?

- Why are there so many trips to the bookshelves on the other side of the room?

- Why is the medical information all out on a bookcase in the other office and not in the same room as the collating?

- Why are all the boxes not opened and supply put on shelves?

- Why isn't there an electric stapler?

- Why not pick the forms from the side of the drawer instead of reaching and standing on tiptoe to get to the back of the drawer?

- Why are the bags back in the room by the file cabinet instead of by the finish table?

Muda of Correction

- Why haven't the old forms been taken out of the file after a change and new forms put in so time doesn't have to be spent on reading to decide which form is the newest from the latest meeting?

The team scrutinized the spaghetti chart, the time study, and the list of MUDA's. Larry then posed the question to them: "Do you suppose that if we removed the MUDA you've listed and changed the layout so that Patty doesn't have to walk half a mile, that this process could be improved by 50 percent?" They all nodded in the affirmative.

Larry continued, "And do you think we can get that 50 percent improved process implemented in the next two days?" Again they nodded even more assuredly this time.

"Okay, we've had a productive day. Let's call it quits and hit this project again in the morning. It's 4:30; we can still get back to our offices and do some catching up on our work. While you're back at your desks and in your offices, you might notice some of these wastes and MUDA in your own work processes. Make a note of them and let's talk about them tomorrow."

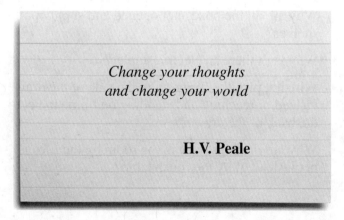

*Change your thoughts
and change your world*

H.V. Peale

Chapter 7

Get Your Customers to Love You & Your Competitors to Fear You

That evening Larry's wife, Sue, had taken their two children to her parents' house, so Larry was a bachelor for the evening. Bob Simms' wife, Lesley, knew about that and invited Larry over for dinner.

Larry arrived just as Bob, Lesley, and their son and daughter were about to sit down at the dining room table. Larry couldn't remember the last time his family of four sat together for dinner. Larry had been keeping late hours at work, and over time, the traditional Smith family dinner together had become a thing of rarity.

Larry thoroughly enjoyed the dinner and was impressed with

the quality of the family discussions as the two kids described their days.

After dinner Larry and Bob went into Bob's home office. Larry loved that office with the paneled walls, leather couch, and big desk. Mostly he admired the idea of having an office with a door—a quiet retreat. Larry did his paperwork on a small table in the corner of his family room. The television, kitchen sounds, and conversations made it tough to concentrate.

Larry sunk into Bob's couch and Bob was leaning back in his high-back office chair behind his desk. "Bob, I want to thank you for having me over for dinner. Without Lesley's invitation, I would have called in for pizza or just stayed later at work. I especially enjoyed sitting with your family. I wish Sue and I could get back to the family having meals together."

Bob leaned back even farther in his chair and put his hands behind his head. "Let me tell you something Larry; you have no idea how appreciative I am that Lesley has made dinner together an ongoing ritual. She has a rule that the family doesn't eat dinner until Dad comes home. Sometimes I don't get in until 8:30 and two starving kids meet me, but Lesley's rule is unbreakable.

"I read an article that said the average American father spends only seven minutes *per week* in conversation with his teenage daughter. Only seven minutes. Think about that statistic. What would a Dad think if his marriage-age daughter came home one night and announced, 'Dad I'm in love with the most wonderful man. He asked me to marry him and guaranteed to spend seven minutes every week speaking to me.' Clearly, when confronted with this humiliating statistic, Mr. Average

American Father would conclude that his management of time needed adjustment and that his priorities were pretty screwed up. That article got Lesley and me thinking and we decided to use the dinner hour to make sure we have quality time together as a family.

"So tell me, Larry, how's your Kaizen event going?"

Larry sat up and leaned forward. "I think it's going okay and we will be able to cut the time in half to assemble the Start Pack, but I'm thinking I picked too simple a process to improve."

"No, Larry, I think you picked a terrific project. It may be simple but it will let you use the most powerful tools in the Kaizen toolbox and it will focus on a strategic weapon—*time*. And isn't your 70-day lead time Jim Brady's biggest headache today?

"Remember that article I was telling you about the man who doesn't spend sufficient time with his daughter and concludes his time management is screwed up—maybe even that he was wasting a lot of time? That's the story of the situation in typical homes, but it's even worse at work. In this Darwinian business climate, organizations that manage their time best will be the fittest that survive. This is true in manufacturing companies as well as service companies.

"I can give you some examples of this. In 1988 the management team of American Standard did a leveraged buyout and were heavily in debt. American Standard became a private company owned by its employees and outside investors with about $4.4 billion in annual sales. Their strategy was to implement Lean with a strong focus on increasing the velocity of all their business processes from order entry through delivery of the finished product to the customer. They were so successful that they were able to deliver the product and receive payment before it was time to pay the suppliers of their raw materials. That meant they actually had 'negative working capital.'

"This isn't a new concept. Back in 1926 Henry Ford said, 'One of the most noteworthy accomplishments in keeping the price of Ford products low is the gradual shortening of the production cycle. The longer an article is in the process of manufacture and the more it is moved about, the greater is its ultimate cost.'

"That's where management of time becomes a strategic weapon. That's when your customers love you and your competitors fear you. Another simple example of this phenomena is McDonald's. When you pay them for your Big Mac, they have your dollars but you can be sure they haven't paid for the meat yet. They can enjoy the 'float' of the money before their suppliers get paid.

"What I'm saying is that I think you picked a very good project. When you're done, not only will you have a better process in place, but also you will have trained a team of practitioners who can take these new tools into improving the processes of their own department.

"I'm sure your project will be a success. But let me warn you. Don't think that just getting back to where you were with your Kaizen in the factory and conducting a bunch of Kaizen events in your service, technical, and administrative departments will automatically evolve into a world-class Lean outfit. It won't happen. All you'll have is isolated victories over waste with no real improvement of your total enterprise.

"You need to start thinking about creating the 'Lean Promotions Office.'"

Students were asked to make a list of people they disliked; those with the longest list were the most disliked.

Anon

Chapter 8

Removing the Muda

The next morning the team was assembled in the HR conference room and ready to attack their problems. They were all drinking coffee and eating the doughnuts Larry brought. Patty swallowed her gulp of coffee and spoke up. "I've been assembling those Start Packs for the past four years and I never realized how much waste there was in the process. I never realized how many of the things I did to assemble those Packs added no value. It really is as though you gave us 'New Eyes.' We've added stuff and taken stuff out of the package over the years but never took the time to study my work making the package from start to finish. It just *evolved* into this process."

Larry responded, "We now have enough data to begin designing our 'future state.' I would like to split this group into three teams. The first team will study the spaghetti diagram and come up with a new layout. The second team will study all the forms and see if we can have some kind of consolidation. The third team will design an inventory control system. I want to work with that third team. I want to show you how to use a Pull System."

Three people gathered all the forms in the Start Pack and were able to eliminate some and combine a group of nine individual forms into a single pamphlet.

A second team studied the spaghetti diagram. One of the major problems was that all the different forms were stored in file cabinets. Patty had to go from one cabinet to the next, opening drawers, looking for the file, extracting the file, and closing the door, over and over again. They made a sketch showing how adding shelves to the wall could eliminate all the MUDA caused by the files. They showed the sketch to Steen who loved the idea and immediately called the maintenance department who promised to have the shelves put up before the end of that day. The team spent the rest of the day moving unnecessary cabinets and equipment out of the area.

On the third day the shelves were in place, the new reduced quantity of forms were located onto those shelves, and the team was ready to do another time study and draw another spaghetti diagram.

Are All These Forms Necessary?   **Forms Eliminated**

Separate Forms Consolidated into One Booklet

Start Pack, Before and After Kaizen

Process Before Kaizen

Process After Kaizen

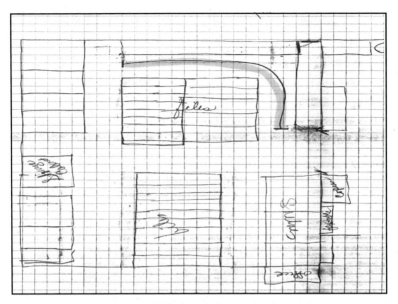

The Spaghetti Diagram After Kaizen.
Only 12 feet of Walking

The team was amazed. Their new method reduced the walking from 2442 feet down to only 12. Patty only took one minute nineteen seconds to complete a pack using the new method that avoided the filing cabinets. That's about a 95 percent improvement.

Steps to Assemble Employee Start Pack	Minutes Before Kaizen	Minutes After Kaizen
Walking	9	0
Searching	2	0
Assembling	12	1 min 19 sec
Copying	4	0
Total	27	1 min 19 sec

Larry had been working with the third team—the inventory control team. "What this department had," Larry explained, "was an inventory control system where you were constantly and unexpectedly running out of forms you needed and at the same time were running out of room for the overflow of forms you didn't need at all. And that's what typically happens in most offices and factories.

"What we need to devise is a 'Pull System.' That is to say that the end customer's demand will pull material through the whole system. So in our case we will say that the new hire is the end customer. When that customer needs a Start Pack, we should have an inventory of completed packs ready to give him or her.

"We need to establish what quantity of completed forms we need to maintain. And then we need to establish at what point the inventory needs to be replenished. The signal to trigger a re-order will be our Kanban* card. Those numbers depend on the anticipated demand for Start Packs and how long it takes to replenish the supply.

"We then need to establish the same set of numbers for all the forms that make up the start pack. What I envision is three levels of inventory—just like in a factory—finished goods, work-in-process, and raw material.

"The finished good would be the finished Start Packs ready to hand to an employee. The work in process inventory would be the forms on Patty's new shelves ready to be assembled into the Start Packs being made. Since the shelves are small, this would be a low inventory number. And the raw material

See explanation of Kanban in appendix

inventory would be the larger quantity of forms that will be maintained in the supply cabinet.

"Let me give you a way to envision all this. Let's say a secretary keeps running out of paperclips at her desk. It wouldn't make sense for her to jam 10 boxes of paperclips into her desk drawer. She would probably keep three boxes of clips there and when she was down to one box, she would get two more from the supply cabinet to get back to her inventory of three.

"In the supply cabinet there would be an inventory level of say twenty boxes and when that got to a replenishment point of eight, an additional twelve boxes would be ordered. All that, of course, depends on how long it would take to get paperclips from the stationery supplier.

"Let's take just one form, try the Long Term Disability Form–the LTD. Get together as a team and come up with inventory levels and replenishment points."

The team came back to him with these values.

Item	Inventory Level	Replenishment Point	Reorder Quantity
Complete Start Packs	6	2	4
LTD Forms on the Shelf	20	5	15
LTD Forms in the Supply Cabinet	60	20	40

LTD Forms in the Supply Cabinet

Inventory 60
Replenish Point 20
Replenish Qty 40

LTD Forms on the shelf

Inventory 20
Replenish Point 5
Replenish Qty 15

Complete Start Pack*
Inventory 6
Replenish Point 2
Replenish Qty 4

*Temporarily stored on floor while shelves were being built.

Larry reviewed the numbers and asked the team to develop the values for the rest of the forms. He explained the Japanese inventory control tool called "Kanban," which means signal. The team needed to create the signal to indicate the replenishment point was reached. He had the team take pink 8½ by 11-inch of paper sheets and position them in the piles at the replenishment points. These sheets—the Kanbans—told the replenishment point, the replenishment quantity, and the source of the replenishment inventory. The bottom photo on page 72 shows the Kanban form next to the pile of completed Start packs on the floor that has only two packs remaining. The Kanban form calls for a replenishment quantity of four. Similar pink Kanbans are shown in the photos of the assembly area shelves and the raw materials cabinet. This became the basis for the HR department inventory control system.

Larry assembled the team. "I want to talk to you about housekeeping," Larry began. "Two of the fundamentals of Kaizen are the requirement for standardization and for good housekeeping. We have developed an excellent process for assembling the Start Packs and for maintaining an inventory of forms. Right now, this is the best process we know of. We need to document this process and assure that everyone who assembles these packs does it this way. We will have 'standardized' the process. Until somebody comes up with a better method, everyone who assembles packs has to do it this way. The way we developed will be documented. It's our standard way. We can't have different people doing the same process differently.

"Housekeeping is a requirement for maintaining standards. Before we did our Red Tag Campaign, this place was a mess. I would like to post photographs of the department now that it's orderly and also of the inside of the supply cabinet to assure that conditions stay this way.

Photo of Neat Cabinet Posted Inside Cabinet Door

Photo of Neat Office Posted on Filing Cabinet

"I hope you folks appreciate what we accomplished in just three days. Although the process we chose to improve may seem trivial in the scheme of things—it's not like we cured world hunger—we achieved remarkable improvements in just three days."

Larry began writing summary numbers on a flipchart. "Okay gang, look at these numbers. The time to assemble a pack was reduced from 27 minutes to one minute and 19 seconds. Our goal was to achieve a 50 percent improvement. We achieved a 95 percent improvement. We reduced Patty's walking distance from 2442 feet to 12. That's a 99 percent improvement. In addition to that, the HR office now looks great and will continue to look great.

"We eliminated the waste of hunting for and searching, as well as waiting for another package to be created, thus reducing the lead time to the customer and user. We have also reduced the stress level of not having what you need when you need it. You reduced the number of things to be ordered or reprinted, plus lowered the levels of inventories so that when changes are needed to update the forms, we have less to throw away or use up before the new forms are used.

"We also saved the company some money. Patty, I understand you work overtime because, while you were spending so much time in this inefficient layout, you weren't able to get all your work done during the normal forty-hour week."

Patty spoke up. "You're right, Larry, I haven't been able to get my work done in a normal eight-hour day. I've been putting in two hours of overtime a day for the past year. At first I appreciated the money but those long hours are getting old. I would gladly give up the overtime pay just to be able to spend more time with my kids in the afternoon.

"There's more money to be saved, Larry. Right now we pay one cent a copy for black and white and eight cents for color. And you know HR departments; everything has to be in color. I think we have cut our department's copier costs in half as a result of this Kaizen."

"Okay, Patty," Larry challenged. "Let's see how much money we saved. I would like you and your team to spend the next half hour calculating how much money we saved."

The team came back with this flip chart:

Category	Savings
Overtime	$19.23/hour x 1.5 (time and one half) x 2 hours/day x 200 days = $11,538
Copier Costs	$.03/copy x 35,000 copies/year x 50% reduction = $525
Total	$12,063

Larry continued, "We demonstrated that by reducing the non-value added portions of Patty's processes we not only made her job easier, we also saved the company a bit of money—and these bits add up. But the real accomplishment is that we now have a team that can be deployed to apply these Kaizen tools to other administrative functions in our company."

John Convery was staring at the numbers on the flipcharts. He stood up from his chair and addressed the group. "I'll tell you the truth, I wanted no part of this exercise. I thought I couldn't afford to take time away from my department during this busy time and I saw no point in focusing on an inconsequential HR process. But this process is no different than every other administrative process in a company. I am very, very impressed with what we've learned here. There's an old saying that goes, *'If you keep doing what you've always done, you'll keep getting what you always got.'* I am very eager to apply these tools to a process in my engineering department that is driving me nuts. The process to change the paperwork resulting from a design change is now taking weeks. This affects product costing, inventory control, production planning, and our suppliers. I'm going to form a team in engineering and have my own Kaizen Event to attack that process."

Barry Moss from Finance then spoke up, "I figured we could improve the start pack process a bit, but I never expected these kinds of gains. I would appreciate it, John, if you would invite me to join your team on the Kaizen Event to improve the engineering change process since my department is strongly affected by it."

> *The power of ideals is incalculable. We see no power in a drop of water, but let it get into a crack in a rock and be turned into ice and it splits the rock. Turn it into steam; it drives the piston of the most powerful engines. Something has happened to it that makes active and effective the power that is latent in it.*
>
> **Albert Schweitzer**

Discussion

From a Lean management standpoint:
What's going on in this chapter?

Larry Smith's team accomplished quite a bit in only three days by using an approach called the Kaizen Event, developed by Toyota. Toyota is the most profitable car manufacturer in the world. As a matter of fact, Toyota's profits are more than all the profits of all the world's car companies combined. Toyota credits the Toyota Production System (TPS) for their success.

TPS wasn't an overnight development. The system evolved over decades and governs every aspect of manufacturing, sales, design, and personnel administration. In the 1970s, Toyota decided they needed a method to quickly infuse TPS into the processes of their key suppliers. This method was the Kaizen Event—a 3 to 5-day exercise to quickly improve a process principally by discovering and eliminating the waste in the process being studied.

When Shigeo Shingo (a Toyota industrial engineer) defined the "7 Wastes" of the Toyota Production System, he opened the company's eyes to where dramatic improvement can be found: Rather than looking primarily at the "value adding" operations that comprise only 10 percent of the elapsed time to provide a product or service, his focus was first at the things that impede the work and make up 90 percent of that elapsed time.

And that's what Larry's team discovered by conducting the MUDA hunt. The MUDA hunt is part of the template defining a Kaizen event. The key template elements deployed in this chapter were:

- The *Red Tag Campaign* to remove clutter.

- The *Spaghetti Diagram* to record and measure unnecessary transportation.

- The *Time and Motion Study* to accurately quantify how time is being expended.

- Imposition of a *Kanban inventory control system* to avoid stock outs and inventory excesses.

- *Standardization* of processes.

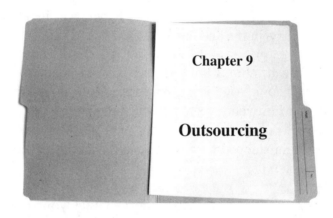

Chapter 9

Outsourcing

Jim Brady's phone rang. It was the receptionist telling him that Mike Bartlett, the outsourcing consultant, was there for their meeting. Brady had been looking forward to this meeting for months. Over the past two years, the price of his raw materials had increased and his competition was forcing him to lower his selling price. He was being squeezed, and he was sick and tired of the complex operations problems at Sonic. The prices Bartlett had quoted to him by phone were almost too good to be true.

Brady's secretary escorted Mike Bartlett into the office. Brady was surprised to see that Bartlett was wearing a suit and tie—unusual in this era of casual business attire.

The men shook hands and sat down across from each other at the conference table. Brady's secretary brought in coffee. Bartlett was stunned by the number of charts Brady had on his wall. Bartlett—a seasoned operations professional—was familiar with that type of executive: the scorekeeper, the menacing after-the-fact judge.

The contrast was significant. Bartlett in his mid forties, very fit, and very affable compared to Brady who was in his early sixties, flabby, puffy, and humorless.

Bartlett began, "Jim, I think I can help your company a lot. I've been helping American businesses go offshore with their production for twenty years. I studied the print package you sent me of your bookshelf speakers and I'm almost positive I can get them shipped here from Asia for less than you now pay for materials.

"I'm sure you've considered the fact that your moving production out of this plant will affect your personnel and even your city. Have you thought about how much business you want to move to Asia?"

"I've thought about that a lot," Brady replied. "Some of the people here have been with me for twenty years. I'm really not sure how much business I want to take out of this plant. I'm thinking of starting out with my highest volume product, the Radiance Series of bookshelf speakers. Depending on how that goes, I'll decide what to do next."

Bartlett was studying Brady and looking around his office. In addition to the dozens of charts, he had an elaborately framed oil painting of himself with his family and dog. The picture appeared to be about twenty years old. Next to the picture were Brady's two college degrees. Bartlett had never seen manufacturing managers hang their degrees in their offices. That is what lawyers and doctors do to comfort their clients.

"It's not a simple decision Jim," Bartlett began to explain. "Many of my clients will move as much as they can to Asia and keep just enough production in America to keep their most valuable and senior people employed. They do this even if the domestic plant does nothing more than just break even.

"One of my Asian sources has a plant in Taiwan. He pays his labor there about $6 an hour. He found a source in Southern China where the labor rate is $1 an hour. He couldn't afford to keep all his production in Taiwan, but he had a loyal workforce there that he needed to protect. He ultimately moved 75 percent of his work to China and manned the Taiwan factory with a crew of people he felt obligated to save. He barely breaks even in that Taiwan operation but he's convinced he did the right thing.

"I'm not sure if China is the right place for you to build your product. We also have to consider Vietnam, Indonesia, Thailand, and India. I've studied the print package and costs that you sent me. Right now your costs for a pair of Radiance bookshelf speakers is $60. That breaks down to $42 for material, $8 for labor, and $10 for overhead. I think a reasonable goal for us is to get the product made in Asia and shipped to you for $30 FOB Asia and after freight and duty we could expect a landed price in this city at $34.

"If we can use your computer, I will show you the web sites of six Asian factories which are equipped to do your type of production."

Brady was stunned as he looked at the images of these Asian factories. He was expecting to see slum buildings with poor lighting, dirt floors, and workers dressed in rags.

All the factory buildings he saw were modern structures, well lit, impressively equipped with the latest robotics and measuring equipment, manned by well-dressed diligent looking workers.

"I'll tell you something Mike; these aren't the images I expected to see. Every one of these factories is more impressive than mine. I wish I had that kind of equipment here. Some of my machinery is twenty years old and these Asian machines on the web sites look brand new."

Bartlett was smiling, "That's the same response I get at every one of these presentations. Asian manufacturing is getting very sophisticated. What I suggest as a next step is a trip to Asia. I will escort you to six facilities there. I don't want to send them print packages unless we're serious about considering them. After the trip, you and I will select two or three of the plants we visit and e-mail print packages for them to quote on. We will also send them product samples. We can expect formal quotes back from them in five days and samples three weeks after that. I'm confident they will meet our $34 goal and that the source we select will deliver products on time and with excellent quality. I've been doing this for a long time and I can promise you that you will be very happy once you outsource your production to Asia.

"If you agree, I'll have my secretary set up appointments for our Asia trip. I think we can visit six plants and be back within five days."

"Let me ask you something, Mike," said Brady. "If I select a Chinese supplier when we're on our trip, how long would it be before I could actually have my production moved there?"

Bartlett scratched his head, thought for a few moments and replied, "Realistically, from the time you give them the go-ahead, you could start receiving product from them within four months."

They shook hands and Brady walked Bartlett to his car. It was a Mazda RX8, a rotary engine sports car. Brady was jubilant as he watched Bartlett's car drive out of the parking lot with the zoom-zoom engine purr.

> *Management is efficiency in climbing the ladder of success. Leadership determines whether the ladder is leaning against the correct wall.*
>
> **S. Covey**

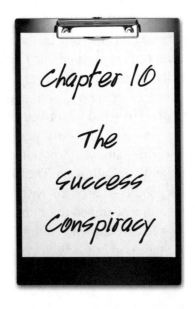

chapter 10

The

Success

Conspiracy

The morning after the Kaizen event in the HR department, Larry arrived at his office at his usual 6:30 a.m. to get a look at the previous day's numbers before his phone started ringing. His routine was to get in early to review the numbers and then take a factory tour to see what was going on with the third shift that started at midnight. Then at 8:00 he held a daily twenty-minute meeting with key staff from production, scheduling, purchasing, and sales.

At 7:30 Larry was returning to his office after his factory tour and was surprised to see Steen Geertsen of HR, Barry Moss of Finance, and John Convery of Engineering standing by his office door.

"What are you three doing here in the middle of the night," Larry asked. "You guys have trouble dragging your asses into work before 8:00 a.m. Something must be up."

"Buy us coffee and we'll tell you what's up," said Barry. The four men walked to the coffee pot in the hallway, poured themselves a cup, and walked together into Larry's office where they sat at his small conference table. Larry had a nice office consisting of his desk, a credenza, and a round conference table with four chairs. His window looked out at the parking lot. His décor was Spartan. The only personal item was a photograph taken of his family the previous summer when they vacationed in Ventura, California. The photo showed four happily smiling tan people—Larry, his wife Sue and their two kids in front of a tent they camped in on the beach. It was an action packed two weeks filled with sailing, ocean kayaking, a trip to Universal Studios in Los Angeles, and a two-day side trip to Tijuana, Mexico.

The only other things on the wall were posters of the latest Sonic loudspeakers. Jim Brady, Larry's boss, kept a clean desk. The only thing on Brady's desk was the paper he was working on. Larry's desk, on the other hand, was covered with not neatly piled piles of papers. The wood surface of the desk wasn't visible. Brady often poked not-so-good-natured fun of Larry for his desk organization and accusingly would say, "A cluttered desk means a cluttered mind," to which Larry would think, but never say out loud, "An empty desk means an empty mind."

John Convery was first to speak. "I want us to move forward on Lean but I would like to do it as a team. Almost every person in the company works for the four of us. We could form the 'Lean Promotions Office' and make sure Sonic becomes a Lean Enterprise."

Larry replied, "You don't know how happy I am to hear those words! Three years ago I implemented Lean practices in my factory and things got a lot better. Brady was one hundred percent behind what I was doing. But being the typical entrepreneur, he is quick to embrace the latest panacea, and just as quick to abandon it in favor of the next one. That guy has the attention span of a flea, but I'm worried that he won't give up on his latest mission to outsource our stuff to Asia. I know how Brady's brain works. He's going to come back from China all excited about a factory he's seen there and announce that we will start outsourcing as of some date a few months in the future. I feel like a clock is ticking for me. I need to get this whole enterprise started on becoming Lean before that date.

"In an ideal world, Brady would have grasped the significance of what Lean had done for the factory. And in that ideal world Brady would then have visibly promoted Lean in his words and actions, not just for the factory but for the whole company. He would have given recognition to managers and employees for initiatives and continuous improvement. He would have encouraged all employees to be involved. We could then possibly have had a company where almost every employee asks the question 'How can we do a better job tomorrow than we are doing today?'

"Well none of that happened. I am very proud of my Lean initiative in the factory but I wish it were company wide. I wish our suppliers were involved. But this is a good chance for us. If we can pull off two Kaizen events with cross-functional teams that really make significant improvements, I think that could light a fire under Brady and get him to embrace and even lead what we're trying to get done. Brady is hung up on the notion that he can cut our costs by 20 percent if we outsource to China. We could cut our costs a lot more than 20 percent if we focus our improvement efforts on reducing our lead times and in removing the non-value added activities in our offices.

"The four of us could be the Lean Promotions Office and act as the steering committee that lays out the game plan, coordinates the events, and makes sure the resources are available. The good thing about Kaizen is that it's a low cost or even a no cost approach for process improvement, so we really don't need Brady at this point."

"I think you're right, Larry," said John. "And I know just the process that needs improvement—my ECR process."

"Excuse me," Steen interjected. "You'll have to excuse this Danish immigrant running the lowly HR department, but you've been bellyaching about your ECR process for months now and I have no idea what an ECR process is."

"Sorry, Steen, let me explain," John replied. "The name stands for Engineering Change Request. When something has to change on a part we either make or buy, an ECR form needs to be filled out. Let's say a certain bracket has two holes in it and we discovered that there have been field failures that could perhaps be avoided if we added a third hole. That sounds like a very simple process doesn't it? But it's not. As a matter of fact, it takes 16 days."

"Sixteen days?" Steen nearly choked on his coffee. "How can it take that long when all you need to do is add a third circle to the bracket drawing? I took mechanical drawing in high school.

How can it take more than fifteen minutes? Sixteen days is ridiculous!"

"You're right, Steen, that sixteen days *is* ridiculous. But you're wrong that all we have to do is draw a circle. First of all we need to decide if adding a third hole would help the problem at all. Maybe it won't. Maybe a third hole will weaken the bracket and make our field failure problem even worse.

"If we do go ahead and add that third hole, we may have increased the cost of the part. If the two holes were pierced with one stroke of a die, then adding a third hole to be punched at the same time wouldn't increase the cost of the part. But we would have to incur the cost of reworking the die set to add that third punch. If on the other hand the holes were manually drilled, then the addition of the third drilling operation would increase the part's cost. The finance department now gets involved. And eventually marketing has to get involved because the increased cost will reduce the margin so maybe the price has to be increased.

"Then we have the issue of the inventory of the existing part in our warehouse. What do we do with them? Use them as is? Scrap them? Manually add a third hole? Now production planning is involved. The finance department has to be involved with that as well. If a vendor supplies the part, we have to notify them. That brings purchasing into the picture. We have drawings of the existing part—the one showing only two holes—all over our building and at our supplier. But if we add a third hole, those drawings will all be incorrect. So my department, engineering—actually Angie in my document control department—has to issue a revised drawing and make sure all the existing drawings get thrown out. So you see, Steen, just adding a five-cent hole to a bracket involves lots of people and, unfortunately, the change process has become unnecessarily complicated over the years. Not only is it taking sixteen days, but the backlog of ECR's is growing faster than we can process them."

Barry was listening intently. "I wish I could stay to finish this conversation. I've got to go now to a meeting of disgruntled accounting office employees. This meeting is about the overtime and Saturdays the office staff is putting in. They're at the breaking point. Our administrative processes are filled with non-value added MUDA. We need to learn how to discover and remove the waste. You can count me in on whatever you guys come up with."

John smacked his hand onto the table. "I say we conduct a Kaizen Event and set a goal to reduce the time it takes to process an ECR from 16 days to 6 days. We can form a cross-functional team with folks from engineering, accounting, HR, and production. I don't see why we couldn't use the same tools we did with the Start Pack in the personnel department.

> *Change of thought makes your behavior change.*
> *Change of behavior makes your habits change.*
> *Change of habits makes your personality change. Change of personality makes your destiny change.*
>
> **Konosuke Matsushita**
> **(Founder of Machusita Electric Corporation known for their Panasonic brand)**

Discussion

From a Lean management standpoint:
What's going on in this chapter?

Sonic Corporation has a dysfunctional Engineering Change System. Every company that designs and makes anything has an Engineering Change System. Once the design is completed, many things could happen to require that the design be changed. Perhaps manufacturing discovered that the part could not be produced as designed. Or perhaps the part had a history of field failures and the design needed to be modified. Or maybe it was discovered that there was a way to make the part less expensive by redesigning it.

Unfortunately, engineering changes are all MUDA. Therefore, all Engineering Change Systems are all MUDA. The reality is that Sonic's ECR system is broken, but in a perfect world, there shouldn't even be an Engineering Change System.

The people at Sonic are attempting to reduce the number of days it takes to process an ECR. The root cause of their problem is that there is any need for ECR's at Sonic. The ultimate goal should be to reduce the number of ECR's, not the time it takes to process them. But that would be a far more complex process improvement project that would have to be subsequent to this one.

The Japanese have three disciplines that tremendously mitigate the need for engineering changes. One discipline is called Quality Functional Deployment and another is called Concurrent Engineering. The third is a simple one—they have customers review the design.

Quality Functional Deployment

Quality Functional Deployment or QFD was developed in Japan in 1975. Simply stated, it is a method of transforming customer needs (also called the *Voice of the Customer*) into engineering characteristics of a product or service. The West became aware of QFD in 1987 after the release of a survey report by the Japanese Society for Quality Control in which it described how QFD was being applied in eighty companies.

Studies have compared product development at Toyota using QFD to product development at General Motors using no QFD. The data show that Toyota had far fewer design changes once the designs were released from engineering and take one-half the time to develop a new model.

Before describing how QFD works, here is a list of the objectives QFD was designed to achieve:

- Completing designs quickly

- Benchmarking competitive product

- Developing new products that set the company apart from the competition

- Analyzing and accumulating market-quality information

- Communicating quality-related information to all processes

- Deploying design intent to manufacturing

- Identifying control points for manufacturing

- Reducing initial quality problems

- Reducing design changes

- Reducing development time

- Reducing development costs

- Expanding market share

Here is how Toyota uses QFD to get the Voice of the Customer into the design. Let's look at the Toyota application of QFD in the development of a car door. Toyota would take a car to a shopping mall and ask people to try opening and closing the door, after which they would conduct a survey. At one such survey, the customers concluded that the ideal car door would have these attributes:

- The electric window would go up and down very quickly.

- The window would withstand horizontal rain blowing at it with a great deal of force without leaking.

- The door would remain open while parked on a steep incline without slamming shut by itself.

- It would take minimum force to close the door securely.

The Toyota people would then get competitive models and measure each of these attributes to see how many of them they could beat. They would then learn that each of these attributes would require a trade-off. For example, in order for the window to go up and down very quickly, a heavy motor would be required. That would increase the weight of the door so that keeping the door open while parked on an incline would be more difficult.

Similarly, if the door were to withstand a heavy gale-force driven rain, the seal thickness would have to be increased, thus making it impossible to make a door that would close securely with little force. Toyota now has a list of trade-offs, each with a cost associated.

Once these data were analyzed and the decisions made, these design specifications would be added to a massive QFD document that included every single aspect of the new Toyota being developed. This document is treated by Toyota as top secret and is kept in a vault. *The document is essentially the new model description.*

Concurrent Engineering

Concurrent Engineering is a method of having information about the downstream issues at design time. An example would be the choosing of a set of parts in the design for which manufacturing equipment is already tooled. A recent study that compared Chrysler to Honda showed that, where Chrysler had hundreds of tools for a certain common automotive sub-assembly, Honda had only six. It was clear that, when Chrysler set out to do a new model design, they started with a blank piece of paper, whereas, Honda would mandate that existing tooling be used in the new model.

The way most products are designed is with a serial process where people from different departments work, one after the other, on successive phases of development. The person at step two doesn't start until the person at step one is finished. Then the person in step three doesn't start until the person at step two is finished. The first problem with this approach is that there is often no reason that upstream processes can't in fact start their part of the development process before the prior step is complete.

In traditional serial development, the product is first completely defined by the design engineering department, after which the manufacturing process is defined by the manufacturing engineering department, etc. Usually this is a slow, costly and low-quality approach, leading to many engineering changes, production problems, product introduction delays, and a product that isn't as good as the competition's.

Concurrent Engineering brings together multidisciplinary teams, in which product developers from different functions work together and in parallel from the start of a project with the intention of getting things right as quickly as possible, and as early as possible.

Such a cross-functional team might consist of representatives of different functions such as purchasing, systems engineering, mechanical engineering, electrical engineering, manufacturing, quality, suppliers, and even customers.

In the Concurrent Engineering approach to development, input is obtained from as many functional areas as possible before the specifications are finalized. This results in the product development team clearly understanding what the product requires in terms of mission performance, environmental conditions during operation, budget, and scheduling.

Concurrent Engineering aims to reduce the number of redesigns, especially those resulting from post-design input from support groups. By involving these groups in the initial design, fewer changes will be needed. The major changes that do occur will occur before the design becomes final. The overall time taken to design and manufacture a new product can be substantially reduced if the two activities are carried out together rather than in series. The reductions in design cycle time that result from Concurrent Engineering also reduce total product cost.

Concurrent Engineering reduces product development time, reduces design rework, reduces product development cost, and improves communications. Examples from companies using Concurrent Engineering techniques show significant increases in overall quality, 30 to 40 percent reduction in project times and costs, and 60 to 80 percent reductions in design changes after release.

If Sonic were a Lean company, they would be using QFD and Concurrent Engineering and the Engineering Change Process would be an insignificant concern. But they're not Lean and their Engineering Change Process is a major headache to the staff.

Chapter 11
Kaizen Event
In Engineering

A cross-functional team of ten was assembled in the conference room. They represented engineering, finance, production, and HR. Larry ran the session. Before the meeting the only thing those invited were told was that they would be spending three days on a continuous improvement team and that it would be a full-time effort. They were to clear their calendars and understand that they would be fully engaged to the point where there wouldn't even be time for them to break away to check email.

Larry insisted that the team not be told that the goal was to reduce the time to process ECR's from sixteen to six days. A key component of the formula for conducting a Kaizen event is the sense of crisis created by the shock of receiving a seemingly impossible goal to be achieved in a ridiculously short period of time. The sense of crisis created assures an atmosphere of creative thinking, resourcefulness, and teamwork.

The first thing Larry did was announce the goal to the team. They unanimously agreed that Larry had lost his mind. The ECR process was ridiculously complex. Several attempts were made in the past to form teams to simplify the ECR process but they were not able to make any headway and were all eventually abandoned. The group feeling today was that it would take months—not days—of work to make any improvement.

Larry asked Angie, the engineering department clerk, to come to the front of the conference room and describe the current process. Angie began, "Until about a year ago, when somebody submitted an ECR to the engineering department to request a change, it was my responsibility to handle the form. I would deliver the form to the engineer responsible for that type of design and then check back with him to see if he approved the change and signed the form indicating his approval. If he approved the change, I would walk that form to the four departments that needed to take appropriate action. That system worked fine while our company was small. I could keep track of the dozen or so forms that were in circulation. But as we grew, I started to lose track of the forms and the system bogged down as the backlog of forms accumulated throughout our administrative system.

"We then came up with the system we use today. After the engineer makes his disposition—to either approve or reject the change—I make five copies of the form and hand deliver them to the five departments that need to take action. Each of those departments needs to indicate on the form what action has to be taken and then they sign the form. These actions are things like whether or not to scrap or rework the existing inventory, whether or not to contact the suppliers, and whether or not the cost or pricing of the product has to be changed. My job is to make sure every department processes every ECR form.

"The process today is out of control. It now takes an average of 16 days for an ECR to get processed. In-baskets are piling up with ECR forms. ECR forms are getting lost. Sometimes an individual is given an ECR form that requires their action. Other times the form is just for their information—not requiring any action. We now hold a weekly ECR review meeting but it's not very productive since nobody knows who's in charge of the overall process.

Exasperated, she exclaimed, "This is by far the worst problem in the company. I used to love my job but now I'm getting blamed for this mess and I don't like coming to work in the morning."

Larry thanked Angie as she returned to plop down in her chair. Not a happy lady.

Larry then began explaining the background and philosophy of Kaizen* and introducing some of the tools and techniques the team would be using.

The first tool was called "Rocks in the Stream." Larry drew a

*Read definition of Kaizen and Kaizen Event in Appendix

sketch on a flip chart and explained that there were reasons that the process was taking sixteen days. These reasons were like rocks in a stream that prevented a straight path across to the other side.

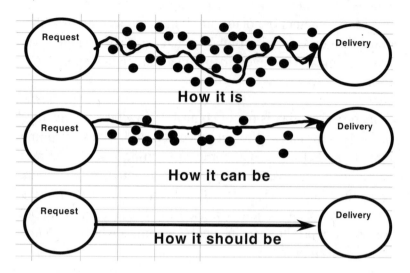

Larry began a brainstorming session and had the team list their "rocks in the stream."

- Inaccurate / incomplete information from requestor
- No champion for process
- No system to track ECR's in process
- System assumes one person has all information
- Too many competing "Hot" ECR's
- No departmental accountability
- Excessive checking in current process
- Lack of delegation by department managers
- Physical location of individuals supporting process
- Lack of cross training
- Lack of validation of original request
- Process has no closure

A heated discussion ensued as the team members began calling out solutions for the problems listed. "Hold on a minute team," Larry cautioned. "Let's not leap to any conclusion yet. Let's not forget the Japanese saying 'Speak with Data' and right now we don't have any data. The next thing I want us to do is draw a spaghetti diagram of the path taken by Angie, who has to distribute the paperwork generated by the weekly Engineering Change Control Meeting. That will give us more data. I've asked Angie to walk the actual path she takes, after the meeting, and simulate the steps she takes. Let's draw a simple sketch as we follow her path."

A team member drew a quick sketch of the office layout and drew a line on the sketch that showed where Angie walked. Her path was from her desk where she logged in her paperwork, to the copier that was in a remote office, and then to the desks of the eight people who needed the new documents. The team then used the sketch to pace off the path taken and convert the paces to feet. They were amazed to learn that Angie was walking 1298 feet every time she did a distribution.

Once again the team started suggesting ideas for office rearrangement, but Larry cautioned them to wait until all the data was collected.

The next team exercise was the Process Map. In most cross-functional processes, it's highly unusual for any one individual in the organization to thoroughly understand the process from end to end. Typically people only understand the parts of the process that they are involved with. They know what papers come to them and whom they came from. And they know what papers they are responsible for and who gets them. That's about all.

Larry pasted four blank flip chart pages on the wall next to each other. He explained that the team was going to construct a process flow document that depicted every step in the ECR process. The first step was to agree on exactly where the process they were studying began and where it ended.

This discussion took nearly half an hour but it was time well spent because defining the boundaries of the process was critical. They agreed that the first step would be the actual filling out of the ECR form. They agreed that the last step would be the complete updating of all relevant documents.

Larry had a stack of four-inch sticky notes. Sticky notes, as shown in the photo on the following page, are self-adhesive four-inch square colored papers. He wrote, "Fill out ECR" on the first sticky and placed it on the upper left of the flip chart pages. He then asked the team what the second step would be. That conversation lasted fifteen minutes as the team debated what actually was the second step. An arrow was drawn between the two steps. Larry explained that the symbol of a diamond on a flow chart represented a decision point and that every decision point step would need to have one arrow coming in to it and two arrows going out since most decision typically have two alternatives: "yes or no." Simply turning those sticky notes 90 degrees made the diamond shape.

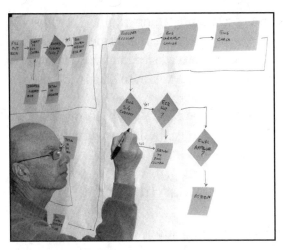

Sticky Notes Used to Build the Process Flow Chart

The team took about two hours to complete the entire process map. They identified fifty-seven separate steps. The team concluded three important things from the exercise: first, that until that morning not one single person in the organization had a clue as to what the total process entailed; second, that nobody had an idea of how ridiculously convoluted the process had become over the years; and third, that there was quite a bit of duplication of effort going on because nobody knew what the entire process consisted of.

Once again the team began suggesting improvements for the process they just mapped but Larry told them to hold off. So that they wouldn't forget these suggestions, he had them start listing on a separate flip chart suggestions to be considered when they redesigned the process.

"Okay team, we're not ready to begin redesigning the process" Larry cautioned. "I know how tempting it is. The idea of Kaizen is to improve the process by discovering the waste in the process and permanently removing it. The most conspicuous waste shown on a process chart is the decisions—the diamonds. But there are a lot more wastes than the decision points. Next we will conduct a MUDA hunt to discover those wastes."

Larry handed them the MUDA hunt forms and gave the team twenty minutes to study the flow diagram and list as many examples of the seven forms of MUDA that they could find.

Muda Hunt Results

Muda of Overproduction
- Why are so many copies of the ECR form distributed?

Muda of Inventory
- Why is there such a large backlog of ECR's in process?

Muda of Conveyance
- Why are there 16 handoffs?

- Why does paperwork have to be distributed to five different departments?

- Why does the original ECR form get returned to the engineering department multiple times?

- Why do ECR's get retuned to originators for incorrect or insufficient information?

Muda of Motion
- Why does Angie do so much walking to process ECR's?

Muda of Processing

- Why do 4 departments have to give separate approvals?

- Why are there multiple rechecks by Document Control and Engineering?

- Why are there decision points in the process?

- Why do we spend so much time in the Change Control Meetings?

- Why do we have multiple ECR's going through for the same issue?

- Why don't planners always understand action required from processed ECR?

Muda of Producing Failures

- Why are so many submitted ECR's not filled in completely?

- Why don't vendors always get notification?

- Why aren't completed ECR's always filled out completely and accurately?

Muda of Waiting

- Why does Document Control need to wait for approval signatures?

- Why do all actions require waiting until next change control meeting?

*The only limit
to our realization of tomorrow
will be our doubts of today.*

Franklin D. Roosevelt

Discussion

From a Lean management standpoint:
What's going on in this chapter?

Larry and his team are busy conducting a Kaizen event designed to improve the performance of the ECR process. The Kaizen approach is to improve processes by discovering and permanently eliminating the waste in the process—the MUDA.

This ECR process is not much of a process. It's more of a *tribal ritual* that has evolved over the years. This phenomenon is illustrated by this poem.

The Calf Path

by Sam Walter Foss

One day thru the primeval wood
A calf walked home, as good calves should;
But made a trail, all bent askew,
A crooked trail, as all calves do.
Since then 300 years have fled,
And I infer the calf is dead.
But still, he left behind his trail
And thereby hangs my mortal tale.

The trail was taken up next day
By a lone dog that passed that way.
And then, a wise bellwethered sheep
Pursued the trail, o'er vale and steep,
And drew the flocks behind him too

As good bellwethers always do.
And from that day, o'er hill and glade
Thru those old woods, a path was made.

And many men wound in and out,
And dodged, and turned, and bent about,
And uttered words of righteous wrath
Because 'twas such a crooked path,
But still they followed, do not laugh,
The first migrations of that calf.
And thru the winding woods they stalked
Because he wobbled when he walked.

This forest path became a lane
That bent, and turned, and turned again.
This crooked lane became a road
Where many a poor horse with his load
Toiled on beneath the burning sun
And traveled some three miles in one.
And thus a century and a half
They trod the footsteps of that calf.

The years passed on in swiftness fleet,
The road became a village street.
And this, before men were aware,
A city's crowed thoroughfare.
And soon the central street was this
Of a renowned metropolis.
And men, two centuries and a half
Trod the footsteps of that calf.

Each day a 100 thousand route
Followed the zig-zag calf about,

And o'er his crooked journey went
The traffic of a continent.
A 100 thousand men were led
By one calf, near three centuries dead.
They followed still his crooked way
And lost 100 years per day.
For this such reverence is lent
To well establish precedent.

A moral lesson this might teach
Were I ordained, and called to preach.
For men are prone to go it blind
Along the calf paths of the mind,
And work away from sun to sun
To do what other men have done.
They follow in the beaten track,
And out, and in, and forth, and back,
And still their devious course pursue
To keep the paths that others do.

They keep the paths a sacred groove
Along which all their lives they move.
But how the wise old wood gods laugh
Who saw that first primeval calf.
Ah, many things this tale might teach,
But I am not ordained to preach.

In studying a process to be improved there are only two metrics
that matter; how long does the process take and how often is it
done right the first time. This ECR process has problems on
both counts. The process takes ridiculously long (sixteen days)
and despite numerous inspections and approval steps there are
still excessive errors.

Most companies rely on some non-value added activities such as inspection to find errors and assure quality. That could be in the form of an inspector at the end of the assembly line whose job it is to find defects. Or in the case of this ECR process, it could be a person in an office whose job is to check over the work of people, see if there are any errors, and perhaps add a signature to show that the work is approved.

Unfortunately, that is not a very good way to assure quality. To illustrate this point, pretend that you are the final inspector in a factory that produces heart pacemakers. And pretend that the following paragraph in the box represents a pacemaker. Pretend that every letter "F" represents a fault or a defect. Your job is to find all the "F's". Give yourself two minutes to find all the F's. See how many you can find.

According to the United Federation of Petroleum Retailers, the files kept by most fuel purveyors lack the organization necessary to run a successful business. This surprised Fred Ferguson of Ferguson's Fuel Depot. He felt that his files were among the best of any filling station he had ever seen. Of course, Fred knew that not all of what he had stuffed into the shoeboxes under his desk was important, but still, frequent and effective filing was the key to his bookkeeping system. Fred, quite insulted, immediately cancelled his subscription to the United Federation of Petroleum Retailer's magazine, the Fuel Filler's Forum, for the remainder of the fiscal year.

If you found them all, you know there were 32. If you didn't find them all, your pacemaker customer will drop dead. It's very unusual to find all 32 F's. Most people miss the F's in the word "of." Studies have shown that on a simple product, inspectors are only able to find 85 percent of the defects.

Besides not being effective at finding defects, there's another problem with relying on inspection as a means of eliminating defects and improving quality. First of all, inspection is expensive (you have to pay the wage of an inspector who adds no value to the product or service). Secondly, the inspectors are not only required to *find* the defects, they are usually also responsible to take the time to *categorize* the defects and even to find the person to *blame* for the defect. Unfortunately, while the inspector is doing all those things, whatever was *causing* the defect is still going on and nobody is addressing that.

At the beginning of World War II, paratroopers were getting killed because their parachutes weren't packed properly and wouldn't open when the ripcord was pulled. The rate of these failures was alarming. The general in charge did a really smart thing. He announced to the parachute folders that every week 10 percent of the parachute folders would be picked at random and be required to jump out of an airplane with a parachute they had just packed. As you can imagine the defect rate plummeted.

Adding a final inspector to the parachute folders would not have done much good. Neither are all the four separate approval steps, in the ECR process. The process has to be designed in such a fashion that errors cannot be made. Consider the process of inserting a floppy disc or memory stick into a computer: You can't insert it incorrectly.

Many leadership teams are more ready to use inspection to assure quality than they are to spend time "mistake proofing" their processes. Leaders are more comfortable to just wait for the inevitable failures and judge whom to blame.

The impediments to improving the velocity of the ECR process are the sixteen handoffs that add unnecessary delays, the multiple approval steps, and the duplication of efforts. By having the team work together to "build" their process map step-by-step with the sticky notes, they are looking at their jobs with "new eyes" and discovering that they have been following the "calf path."

If you want something you never had,
you've got to do something
you've never done.

Tony Roberts

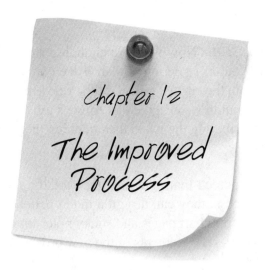

Chapter 12

The Improved
Process

Larry had the spaghetti diagram, the rocks in the stream flow chart, and the MUDA hunt summary taped to the front wall of the conference room. He addressed the group, "There are still two pieces of data missing. It's not enough to say, 'the current process results in too many errors.' We need to 'Speak with Data.' Before we continue we need to go back into a few month's records and quantify the error rate. The other thing we need to quantify is 'touch time.' By that I mean how many minutes are actually spent by the people who touch the ECR. That's the only value added part of the ECR process. Everything else is MUDA."

An hour later the team returned with the astounding discovery that 70 percent of the ECR's for the last four months had to be returned to the originator for insufficient data. The team used their stopwatch to time people as they processed three typical ECR's and learned that it only took 11.6 minutes per ECR. What an incredible discovery; it took 11.6 minutes to process an ECR but it took sixteen days to get through the system from start to finish.

Larry then said, "Now we have enough data to redesign the process. Wouldn't you agree that, if we could eliminate the MUDA from the current process, the cycle time would drop a lot? And wouldn't you agree that Angie's job of making ECR copies, distributing them and then tracking them down is ripe for redesign?"

The group agreed that, now that they totally understand the current process, they can design a much better one. Using a fresh set of flip-chart pages and sticky notes they constructed a new process. The elements of the new process consisted of:

- The current paperwork form could be made into an on-line form to be emailed. That would eliminate all the copies. Angie could then distribute the forms *only* to the individuals who need to take action.

- A big problem was the current form was confusing and 70 percent of the time it wasn't completely filled out, requiring Angie to return it to the originator. A new on-line form could be designed so that it couldn't be forwarded unless it was completely filled out.

- It was agreed that the weekly meetings were

chaotic, mostly because the ECR process didn't have a "champion." The engineering supervisor was designated as the new King of ECR's and his "metric" would be to achieve the six-day goal.

- The current flow chart had sixteen diamonds— that's sixteen decision steps. Decision steps are all MUDA. The new process had only ten.

- The copier easily could be moved closer to Angie's desk to reduce her MUDA of transportation.

The team agreed that the new process could cut the time down from sixteen to six days. They all thought that since this was such a pressing problem that they could get the new on-line form designed and implemented within one month.

Larry had them construct a "Work Plan" in the form of WHAT-WHO-WHEN. This plan listed all the steps required to implement the new process and who would do it on what date. John Convery, as head of engineering, said that he would champion the new process implementation.

While Convery was working with them on the Work Plan, Larry walked down the hall to Jim Brady's office. Jim was looking at photos of the six factories in China he was about to visit. "Hey, Jim," Larry interrupted, "Can you spare a few minutes and join us in the conference room? We just completed a three-day Kaizen Event. Our team studied the ECR process and came up with some great improvements. It would be appreciated if you could listen to what they came up with and maybe give them some recognition for a job well done."

Brady was half listening and was still looking at the photos on his desk while Larry spoke. Larry wished he could take Brady by the earlobe and pull him into the conference room.

Brady reluctantly rose from his chair while still looking at the photos and followed Larry into the conference room. Larry addressed the team: "Ladies and gentlemen, I told Jim what you've been working on these past three days and he wanted to see what you've done. Angie, why don't you take Jim through your project."

Angie walked to the front of the room and explained the spaghetti diagrams, the MUDA hunt, and the flow charts. She then said, "Mr. Brady, you have no idea how screwed up our ECR process was. It was taking sixteen working days—that's three weeks to make the simplest design change. It was affecting our suppliers, our shop, and worst of all, our new product introduction schedule. We've been putting *patches* on the process for years but never really made it much better. Larry taught us these great Kaizen tools this week and in only three days we've designed a process that should reduce the cycle time from sixteen days down to six. That's a 63 percent improvement."

Brady was savvy enough to say the right thing. "Well that is very impressive. We've been struggling with that damn process for years. You all should be really proud of yourselves." Larry could tell that Brady's mind was someplace else and had barely paid attention to what Angie was saying. Brady thanked the team and excused himself to return to his office. Convery followed Brady to his office and while they were walking down the hallway Brady commented to Convery, "I know you guys are trying hard to improve the administrative processes and I appreciate your efforts. But our customers are hammering me and I have to do something different. Outsourcing to China might be just what we need. *Maybe* we can turn things around here by expanding our Lean initiatives. I'll try to keep an open mind."

Larry was sorry he brought Brady in but figured that the team didn't know Brady well enough to know that his mind was elsewhere. In China.

It was now 4:45p.m. on the third day of the Kaizen event. Larry could see that the team was tired from the intensity of the activities. He addressed them, "I want to ask you guys a question. How many of you on day one thought you would be able to design a process that would cut the ECR cycle time to six days?" Nobody raised his or her hands. Angie offered, "This is the fourth time I had been invited to join a team to improve the ECR process. But this is the only team to come up with anything useful. I have no doubt that this will tremendously improve our process. One thing for sure—I won't have to walk 1298 feet every time I need to make a distribution. We moved the copier next to my desk and then simulated the new process. Now I'll only have to walk 142 feet. And another thing: I can't believe how much time has been wasted over the years by my having to return incomplete ECR forms to originators."

I think the Kaizen process is terrific and I can see how it can be applied throughout our company."

Larry thanked Angie and began a new topic "We have been talking about two important concepts: *Continuous Improvement* and *Speaking with Data*. This event to improve the ECR process isn't a one-time thing. Our efforts to improve the ECR process have to keep going on. I want to show you a useful charting technique. The first chart is a simple way to see how our process improvements are trending.

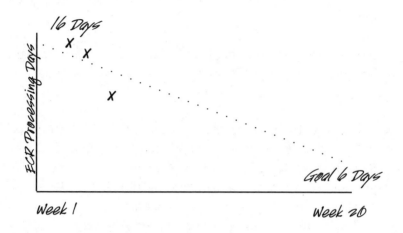

Larry drew this simple trend chart on the flip chart. "The dotted line will represent our projected rate of improvement and each week we can put an "X" to see where we actually are.

"One of the big differences between a factory and an office is that in factories we are always measuring things, but you hardly see that in offices. If you go through our factory you will see charts measuring things such as how many pieces were produced, how many defects were made, how many of our shipments were on time. You don't see that sort of focus on measurements in the administrative areas. This chart will be the beginning of our initiative to start measuring administrative processes.

"The second chart I want to explain is called a Pareto chart. Vilfredo Pareto was an Italian economist who theorized in 1906 about the unequal distribution of wealth in Italy. He said that

80 percent of Italy's wealth was owned by only 20 percent of Italy's population. He was correct and it's probably true with most countries even today. In the 1940s Dr. Joseph Juran was one of the management scientists sent to Japan by our government to help with their industrialization. He had an approach to problems solving called 'The vital few and the trivial many.' He explained his approach as the 80-20 rule, the origin of which he credited to Pareto.

"He explained that 20 percent of something is always responsible for 80 percent of the results. Some examples are: 20 percent of a company's defects account for 80 percent of their problems, 20 percent of the products provide 80 percent of the profits, 20 percent of the salesmen produce 80 percent of the sales, 20 percent of the staff cause 80 percent of the problems, or 20 percent of the products take up 80 percent of the warehouse space.

"The point is that we need to focus our efforts on the vital few, not the trivial many. We need to focus our attention on what matters."

Larry had the team estimate how many days of delay each the form of MUDA was causing and he created a Pareto chart to depict the situation.

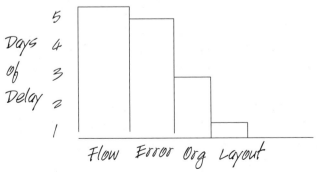

Chapter 12

"The third chart we need is one to show how we will now focus on *the vital few*. This chart helps illuminate the point that we need to focus on flow and errors to get the most value for our efforts. Time spent on the organization and the layout would be better spent elsewhere."

Larry took a fresh flip-chart page.

Problem	What	Who	When
Flow	Put System Online	G.B.	Week 4
Errors	Redesign Form	E.F.	Week 3
No Organization	John Now Responsible	J.C.	Week 1
Too Much Walking	Rearrange Office	A.Z.	Week 1

"This third chart is probably the most important for a number of reasons. Most companies will create a 'to-do' list and assign things to individuals but they forget to write down the problem they were trying to solve. Sometimes the solution doesn't work because folks forgot what problems they were trying to solve.

"The other thing we show on this chart is who is responsible. I once saw a poster that read, "Search all the public parks and you'll never find a monument to a committee." For some reason in our company, we always assign tasks to committees or teams. No one single person then feels a sense of responsibility. That's one of the reasons we have such a poor history of solving problems. Now we have a chart that will be conspicuously posted to show *who* is responsible for *what* and *when* it is expected.

"We now have all the information we need to create a one-page form to post in a conspicuous place so that, at a glance, anyone can see how we are trending with our improvement efforts, what the causes of our problems are, and what we are doing about them. We can update the chart weekly to keep it current. I'll take these three flip-chart pages and make up a one page 8 ½ by 11 form."

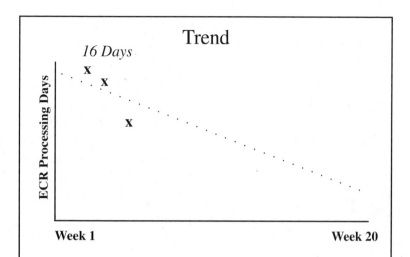

Trend

16 Days

ECR Processing Days

X
X
X

Week 1   Week 20

Pareto Chart

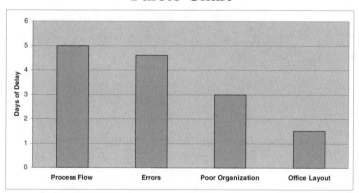

Days of Delay

6
5
4
3
2
1
0

Process Flow   Errors   Poor Organization   Office Layout

Actions Planned

Problem	What	Who	When
Flow	Put System Online	G.B.	Week 4
Errors	Redesign Form	E.F.	Week 3
No Organization	John Now Responsible	J.C.	Week 1
Too Much Walking	Rearrange Office	A.Z.	Week 1

The day was coming to an end and it was time for Larry to wrap things up. "I'm enormously proud of this team and you should be proud of what you have accomplished these three days. As a sign of my appreciation, I'd like to take you all out to a proper dinner tomorrow night."

Larry Smith, John Convery, Steen Geertsen, and Barry Moss as representatives of the management team each shook the hands of the team members and thanked them for what they had accomplished.

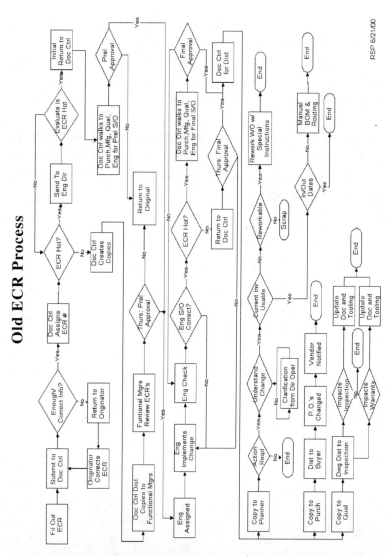

The sticky notes version of the flow chart was reproduced using Microsoft Visio. The flow chart was used to conduct the MUDA hunt to identify sources of waste such as redundant activities, unnecessary approval steps, excessive decision points and avoidable errors.

New ECR Process

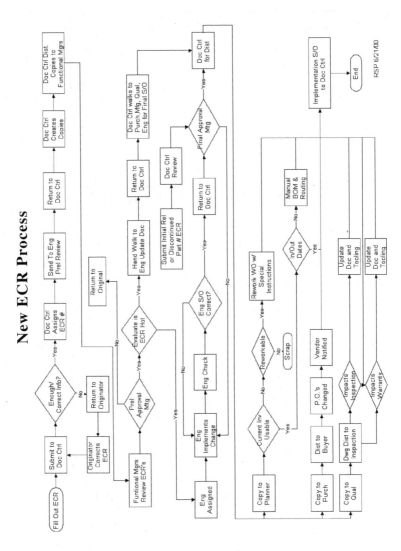

RSP 6/21/00

The new ECR process uses a simplified form to be accessed via email. This eliminated the errors with the previous forms and reduced the number of unnecessary copies of the form. The only hard copies of the form were the ones delivered to people who needed to take action.

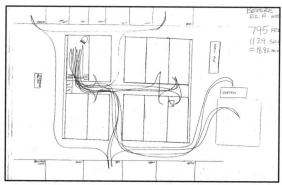

Spaghetti Diagram of Old Method

In the original method, Angie copied every form and delivered the copies to four departments whether or not their action was required. 70 percent of the time the forms were incorrectly filled out—information was missing.

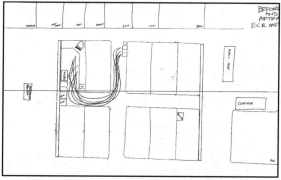

Spaghetti Diagram of New Method

The spaghetti diagram of the new method shows that the only hard copies made are for those individuals who need to take action. Angie scans the original and emails the scanned image to those individuals who need to be aware of the change but are not required to take any action. The hard copies requiring actions are put into the mail slots of the intended recipients. The walking required was reduced from 1298 feet to 142.

The problem in my life and other people's lives is not the absence of knowing what to do, but the absence of doing it.

Peter F. Drucker

Discussion

From a Lean management standpoint:
What's going on in this chapter?

The principal tool used by the team was the process flow chart that they used as the basis of their MUDA hunt. The tool in vogue today is the Value Stream Map.

The Value Stream map as explained by Mike Rother and John Shook in their 1998 book, *Learning to See,* offered analytical tools that simply were not available in older tools. Value Stream Maps offer visualizations of a company that had never before been available. The Value Stream Map, like the process flow chart, is a graphic depiction of the steps in a process but, unlike the process flow chart, the Value Stream Map captures additional data:

- Production flow is recorded from the raw material supplier to the end customer.

- Inventory levels at each level in the value stream are quantified.

- Cycle time, setup time, scrap, rework, and utilization are shown for each process step.

- Information product flow is shown superimposed on the physical product flow.

- All delays in the process are noted. Delays cause lead times to be extended.

The other day I went to the Quick Lube shop to have the oil changed in my car. The sign in front of the building read, "10 minute Oil Change." I waited on a line in my car for 20 minutes before they began the oil change process and that really did take only ten minutes. But I spent 30 minutes in total there (20 minutes on their line and then ten minutes to have my oil changed.) The "Service Lead Time" was 30 minutes but the Value Added time was only ten minutes.

A similar analysis is shown in the Value Stream Map below in which a doctor's appointment is graphically represented. This medical clinic believes that their patients spend five minutes making a phone call to get an appointment and then ten minutes with the doctor. That's only 15 minutes. But as far as the patient is concerned they had to spend a total of 7 days, 1 hour and thirty-five minutes to get those ten minutes with the doctor.

Doctor's Appointment

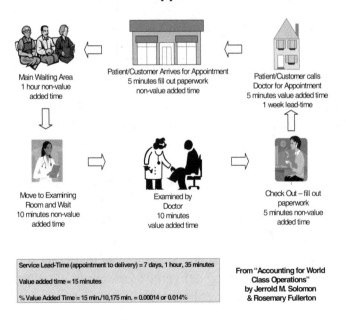

Main Waiting Area
1 hour non-value
added time

Patient/Customer Arrives for Appointment
5 minutes fill out paperwork
non-value added time

Patient/Customer calls
Doctor for Appointment
5 minutes value added time
1 week lead-time

Move to Examining
Room and Wait
10 minutes non-value
added time

Examined by
Doctor
10 minutes
value added time

Check Out – fill out
paperwork
5 minutes non-value
added time

Service Lead-Time (appointment to delivery) = 7 days, 1 hour, 35 minutes

Value added time = 15 minutes

% Value Added Time = 15 min./10,175 min. = 0.00014 or 0.014%

From "Accounting for World
Class Operations"
by Jerrold M. Solomon
& Rosemary Fullerton

The following Value Stream Map shows the processes in a company, starting with their information flow at the top in which the customer order is entered, the daily hot list and daily ship schedule are generated, and the order for raw material from the steel supplier is issued. The flow through the factory is then depicted and culminates in the daily shipment to the customer.

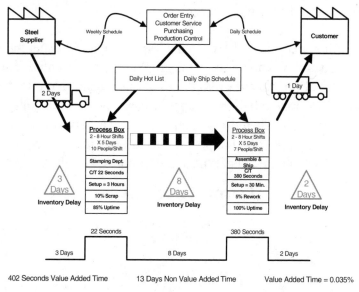

The steel supplier in this example makes a delivery as shown by the truck icon every two days. The raw steel sits in inventory for three days before the stamping department uses it. The three triangles on the map show the inventory delays. The Process Box for the stamping department shows that ten people work there on two eight-hour shifts, five days per week. The stamping cycle time (C/T) is 22 seconds, setups take 3 hours, they have a 10% scrap rate and the machines are usable 85% of the time. Then the stamped parts sit in inventory for a total of 13 days before being delivered to the assembly department where that Process Box shows that the assembly and shipping departments also works 2 shifts a day for 5 days, have a cycle time of 380 seconds, setups take 30 minutes, they have 5% rework and the department is available 100% of the time. The finished part is then put into inventory where it remains for two days before it gets shipped.

The horizontal line at the bottom of the map separates the value added time from the non-value added time as the products flow from the left side of the map towards the right. Value added time is shown on the two "bumps". Stamping takes 22 seconds and assemble and pack take 380 seconds. These are the only value added activities. The 3 days prior to stamping, the 8 days sitting in inventory prior to assembly and the 2 days waiting to be shipped are all non-value added.

This Value Stream Map shows that it takes this company 13 days to do 402 seconds of work. Value added time is only 0.035% of the total time.

This is a useful tool to help discover where the non-value added time is so the velocity of the total process—from receipt of raw material to delivery to the customer—can be improved.

You get what you settle for.

**Line spoken by Susan Sarandon as Louise
in the 1991 film, *Thelma and Louise***

The Lean
Promotions Office

After the team left, Larry spoke to his three peers. "As you can see, Brady isn't exactly enamored with our Lean implementation. But I think it's our only hope of keeping this facility and our jobs here. With Brady so intent on outsourcing, I'm starting to feel like my clock is ticking and the clock is attached to a time bomb. We need to improve our administrative areas before the bomb goes off.

"Brady is hung up on the idea that getting our products from China will save 20 percent. I'm convinced that we can save more than that by keeping our focus on removing non-value work from our offices. Let's do a rough calculation of how much money was saved by removing the waste from the ECR process."

Larry stood in front of the flip chart to begin making a list. "I think, by far, the biggest savings will be that we freed up the design engineers from wasting time on ECR's that they can now devote to developing more new products. Having more new products would be worth a lot of money to us but the amount would be hard to calculate. Another thing that would be hard to calculate is how much of our 70-day lead time was caused by the ECR delays.

One thing we can calculate is how much overtime we've been spending because of the ECR process. The group estimated that, between engineering, accounting, and materials, an average of one hour a day, six days a week was being spent by eleven people associated with ECR-related issues. They also recalled three incidences in the past year when parts had to be scrapped or reworked because of errors incurred in the ECR process. The value of all that waste was $70,000."

Larry summarized that finding on the flip chart.

Category	Savings (Avoidance)
Overtime	11 people x 6 hours per week x $19/ hour x 1.5 (time and one half) x 50 weeks = $94,050
Scrap & Rework	$70,000
Total	$164,050

Barry then suggested, "By having just one Kaizen event we saved the company $164,050. Why don't we just have a bunch of Kaizen events in each of our four departments? The four of us control almost the entire company. We can improve every single process and remove all the waste from our company and save a lot more than the 20 percent Brady imagines we can save by getting product from China."

"I don't think that's such a hot idea, Barry," replied Larry "All that would give us is isolated victories over waste without improving the overall enterprise. We need a carefully laid out plan to assure that all our efforts are directed at accelerating velocity of our processes and improving the 'right-the-first-time' metric with a relentless focus of eliminating MUDA –waste.

"More Kaizen events certainly will be part of our strategy but that means that each event will need to be followed up on and new events will need to be coordinated—enterprise wide. The four of us need to establish the Lean Promotions Office, the LPO.

"I have a vision for what this company can look like and our LPO fits into that vision. First and foremost we need to develop a Value Stream Map of our current situation. It's a very simple graphic representation of every step in our company process, starting with the receipt of an order through to our customer receiving their finished product. Three years ago my friend Bob Simms taught me about Kaizen and gave me 'new eyes.' He showed me that it took nineteen days to go from raw material to finished product even though the actual time to make the product was only about twenty minutes. Using Kaizen as our Lean tool we reduced the nineteen days to three days. Since then that has crept back up to eight days. I have no idea today what the lead time is from the time the customer places the order until they receive that product. That has got to be the focus of our Lean initiative. That affects cash flow and customer retention.

"Once we have that 'Current State' Value Stream Map we can design the 'Future State' Value Stream Map and use that to initiate a series of Kaizen events all directed at achieving the 'future State'. In my vision, every department in our company will be conducting Kaizen events. I picture every person in this company having an attitude that asks, 'how can I do a better job today than I did yesterday?'

"In the factory, I have every department post their key metrics on a bulletin board that is updated daily. These metrics include things such as schedule adherence, quality level, number of good pieces produced, and pieces per person per day. I tour the plant every morning and have an hourly operator from each department explain yesterday's numbers and tell me today's plan. I think we can do the same thing with our office departments. Which reminds me, besides our cost problems, Brady is most concerned with our long lead times. We need another member for our Lean Promotions Office to help attack that issue. We need Marketing to be represented. I think I can convince Janet Kass, their director, to join us.

"We can have every department develop the key metrics that will lead us to achieving the 'future state.' We can then help them conduct their own Kaizen events to remove the waste from those processes that drive their key metrics. Each department will then have a bulletin board with what I call their 'dashboard of metrics.' I use the term dashboard because in a car we are given only six gages to give us the data we need for driving. The car companies could provide us with dozens of gages to show things like manifold pressure and exhaust gas temperature but those are of no use. That's what we need to do in our company. Each department must develop its own dashboard of metrics and focus only on the important process indicators. And it's important—very important—that these metrics must directly connect with the overall goals and objectives of the company.

"Three years ago Bob Simms conducted our first Kaizen event in the factory that yielded stunning results. After that I was able to conduct my own Kaizen events. I used similar tools in the factory that I used this week on this administrative Kaizen. If we're going to have Kaizen events going on in every department, we will need to train Kaizen event leaders. That's the way Kaizen is typically used for Lean implementations. The company hires a *sensei* – the Japanese word for *teacher.* The *sensei* conducts a few Kaizen events and after that the company continues to conduct their own Kaizen events. The *sensei's* task is sort of a technology transfer agent and helps accelerate and guide the process while avoiding the usual pitfalls."

Larry then reached into his back pocket and took out a folded piece of paper. "I've written a draft charter for our Lean Promotions Office. My suggestion is that our very first task will be to map our processes to show current state and future state. This will show us where the Kaizen events will have to take place and will allow us to prioritize and schedule them. At that point we will be able to show *quantitatively* what our future state will be. We will also be able to show exactly how we will get there, by when, and exactly who has to do what.

- The LPO will schedule all future Kaizen events and coordinate the logistics and resources the events will require. For example, in order for this ECR event to be a success we need to get our programmer to immediately begin programming the online form. Since the programmer works for Barry, that's no problem.

- After each Kaizen event, the LPO will have to lead postmortems to glean *lessons learned* and to make sure the to-do lists are being addressed.

- Once we have a proliferation of Kaizen events, it will be the job of the LPO to keep everyone in the company informed about improvement results. Maybe we will have to start a company Kaizen newsletter or establish a Kaizen bulletin board in the cafeteria.

- It would probably be a good idea to share these results with our customers and suppliers. We could invite them to special tours and to Kaizen team report-outs.

- I think our LPO team should take a weekly tour of the entire facility and have employees present to us the results shown on their departmental bulletin boards. That will give us a chance to give them recognition and a chance for them to ask us for any additional resources to help them improve even more.

- A high point for the Kaizen event is what's called the 'report out.' It's where the Kaizen team gets to present the results of their intense week to an audience of peers, supervisors, managers, and executives. It's an opportunity to celebrate the completion of a successful and difficult project during an intense period. It's also an opportunity to show off. Our job will be to invite the appropriate people and maybe arrange for certificates or thank you gifts for the team.

- The main thing we need to do is to keep the momentum going and make sure that all improvement activities are focused on achieving the 'future state' we want.

- If we do this in a coordinated and highly communicative way—everyone singing together in harmony—we will surely have an unmatched success that will let us compete in ways we never thought possible before…and make more money for the company at the same time.

And with that the Lean Promotions Office was created. That night was the first time in weeks Larry was able to leave work and drive home with the feeling that there was a chance of keeping his job. But he started thinking about writing a new resume anyway. Just in case.

> *Life is not easy for any of us.*
> *But it is a continual challenge and it is up*
> *to us to be cheerful and be strong,*
> *so that those who depend on us can draw*
> *strength from our example.*
>
> **Rose Kennedy**

Discussion

From a Lean management standpoint:
What's going on in this chapter?

In the book *Lean Thinking* by Womack and Jones, they describe a four-step action plan to implement the Lean enterprise. The steps are:

- Find a change agent

- Obtain core knowledge

- Seize or create a crisis

- Map your processes to determine *the current situation* and to envision the *future state*.

In our story, Larry has stepped up to the bar and has been accepted by his peers as the change agent. He has the core knowledge and is transferring his knowledge and experience about Lean.

The crisis doesn't need to be created; the company is contemplating moving the work to China. A crisis helps create *The Teachable Moment*. The next step is to begin working on the Value Stream Maps that will illuminate their situation.

This company is typical in their approach to improving things. They focus on the latest thing that went wrong and try to fix it. The problem with that approach is that, by reacting to the latest exceptional issue, they never spend time on solving problems that are the root cause of the company's poor performance. As a result the *real* problems never get solved.

*No problem can withstand
the assault of sustained thinking.*

Voltaire

Chapter 14

Kaizen of the Hiring Process

Larry was at his desk, deep in thought, when Steen Geertsen popped through the door. "Hey, Larry, got a minute?" Larry usually was annoyed by interruptions when he was working at his desk but this time he welcomed the break. "I always have a minute for Danish refugees. What's up Steen?"

Steen had two rolled-up flip-chart pages with him. He taped one up on Larry's office wall and began explaining. "Yesterday at my weekly staff meeting, we had a long discussion about the frustrations we were having recruiting qualified candidates. They agreed that it was one of the greatest sources of aggravation and disappointment for them. We had a feeling that the 'time-to-hire' cycle was a long one, but none of us had ever bothered to chart the process out to see just how long it really took and what all the steps were. So I decided to carve out a few hours and do a mini-Kaizen event in my office to see how we can improve the 'time-to-hire' process.

"We drew this process map. Until we drew this map, none of us had any idea that, if everything went right, the average time to hire was more than three months. Sometimes it has taken us over six months.

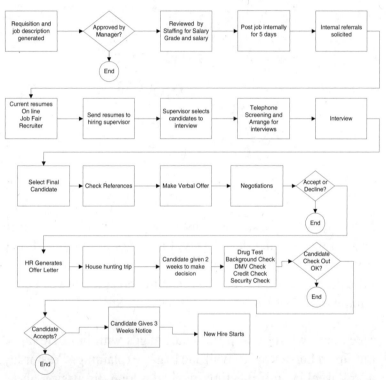

After completing the map we did a MUDA hunt. I typed up what we discovered."

Steen handed Larry the page with the MUDA hunt results.

Muda of Overproduction

- Why do we have so many resumes of unqualified candidates?

Muda of Conveyance

- Why do all our staff members doing interviews have to be in town at the same time?

- Why do candidates have to travel here for initial interviews?

Muda of Waiting

- Why do we wait for internal referrals?

- Why do we wait for job posting results?

- Why do we wait so long for the candidate to get a trip to visit here?

- Why do we wait for our staff to be here to interview candidates?

- Why do we wait for the staff's interview evaluations?

- Why do we give candidates two weeks to decide if they accept our position?

- Why do we allow candidates to give three weeks notice to their current employers?

Muda of Processing

- Why do candidates drop out at the end, causing us to repeat the whole process to finds a new candidate?

Muda of Producing Failures

- Why can't we find better candidates?

- Why do so many candidates drop out after visiting our town?

Steen continuted, "Once we had our process map done and the list of MUDA's we had a very productive brainstorming session that I'm positive will cut our average "time-to-hire" period in half.

Let me tell you what we've come up with that we will immediately implement."

Steen walked up to the flow chart he had taped on the wall and pointed to the first box. "Here's one of our biggest priorities, *Requisition and job description generation.* We are terrible at writing a job description. The hiring manager either takes an old job description from the files or, if we're hiring somebody to replace a person who was fired, reworks the old job description to avoid a similar failure mode. These job descriptions are hardly ever comprehensive enough.

"We decided that we could cut out a lot of unnecessary interviews if we had a clearer understanding of the job requirements up front. My department, until now, had very little involvement with the development of the job description. From now on, I'm going to personally facilitate that process.

"Another problem is that so many people are involved in evaluating the candidates we present that there isn't a clear understanding of what the priorities of the candidate's qualifications should be. I can't be expected to find an accounting supervisor who can speak Swahili and play the violin. We never bothered to get a consensus from the interviewing team about the *priorities* of the qualifications. Everything can't be a number one priority. We would like an accounting supervisor with ten year's experience, with knowledge of our industry and with expertise in computer systems. What if we had to give up one of these qualifications? Which one can we give up? We need to make these decisions up front.

"If I can facilitate the development of the priorities and help develop a list of the job's success factors, I can save several weeks of wasted time with candidates we shouldn't bother with."

Steen then pointed to the fourth box, *Post jobs internally for 5 days*. "Here's a program that we haven't had much luck with. I can't recall more than a handful of times that we had success with this."

Steen then pointed to the fifth box, *Internal referrals solicited*, and explained, "We have a program here to encourage our employees to submit the names of people they know who may be qualified for the job. If one of those candidates is hired, the employee who made the referral is given $1000. We started that program years ago to save on recruiting expenses. Unfortunately, we haven't been very successful with referrals and we waste ten days with it. So from now on, instead of waiting one week for the referrals and an additional week for internal posting before we start outside recruiting, we are going to do all three activities simultaneously. That will take two weeks off the cycle.

"Once the hiring supervisor gets to look at the resumes we send him and he selects possible candidates, the real MUDA begins. Our policy has always been that, after a brief phone interview, we bring the prospective candidates to our facility for face-to-face interviews with the staff. This presents some problems. First of all the candidate needs to schedule time when he can get away from his job for a day. Then there's the problem with our staff. It's hard to find a day when the four to six decision makers doing the interviews will be in town. This scheduling can add a week to the schedule. Our solution is to no longer wait until all our staff is here to do the interviews. From now on, if a secondary interviewer can't be here in person, they will do the interview via video conferencing. We don't have video conferencing equipment here but we can get it done at a local service for $150 an hour.

"The other thing we thought of was to do these interviews on weekends. It makes it easier for the candidate to get away and, since we're usually hard pressed to fill the openings, we don't mind spending a Saturday morning here.

"One of our biggest frustrations is getting the feedback from the folks who do the interviews. We give them each a form to fill out to summarize their assessment. The problem is some of these guys hold onto the forms for a week before we get to see them. From now on we want those forms twenty minutes after the interview takes place. That can cut another week off the cycle."

Steen pointed to the box, *Select final candidate*. "We spent a lot of time discussing this box. I can't tell you how many times we select the final candidate, make an offer, invite him out to do house hunting and when we think we're about to hire him, he declines to join us. Maybe he gave his boss two week's notice and they talked him into staying. Or maybe he was fortunate enough to be interviewing at two companies and he played one offer off the other. When the candidate drops off at the end of the process we have to start over from the beginning. It's a colossal waste of time and very discouraging to the staff.

So from now on we are going to try to always have two final candidates; a number one and a number two."

Steen then pointed to the box, *House-hunting trip*. This has been a problem in the past. The last candidate we made a job offer to wanted to bring his wife and kids to check out the town. Nothing wrong with that. We had a local realtor show them houses. The problem was that she showed them houses that cost over $1 million and this fellow would only be able to buy a $600,000 house. We lost that candidate and had to start from square one. Six weeks wasted.

"From now on we're going to be very careful who shows our candidates around and we will make sure they are prepared with the right information.

"Another area where we waste a lot of time is in waiting for the candidate's decision. Up until now we gave them ten days to decide if they will accept our offer. From now on we will cut that to four days. Many candidates want to give their current employers three to four week's notice. We're going to cut that down to two weeks.

"One of the things we've learned over the years with recruiting is that time is of the essence. Once the process starts to drag out, momentum is lost and as you know, things happens. We can implement all these changes immediately and we think we can reduce our cycle time and also make things a lot easier for our staff as well as for the candidates.

"I tried to calculate how much money this new process will save us. The big savings, of course, is time. With the time my HR department saves, we can devote our energy to making

Chapter 14

this a more efficient company. Last year we had four candidates turn us down after their house hunting trips here. When we added up the hotel and airline expenses for those trips for the candidates and their spouses, it totaled up to $8,400. That's not a fortune but it's another little bit to add to the 20 percent amount that Brady thinks he's going to get by outsourcing.

"It's amazing how little time it took us to come up with all these improvements to our recruiting process. The Kaizen approach of improving processes by eliminating waste is one of the best tools I've learned."

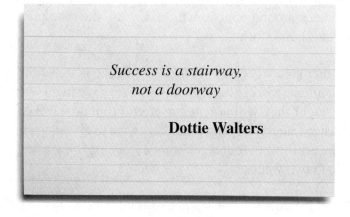

Success is a stairway,
not a doorway

Dottie Walters

152

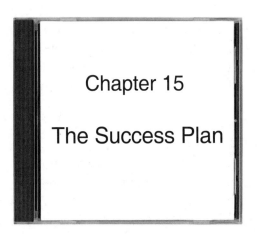

Chapter 15

The Success Plan

Despite numerous attempts to hold their first Lean Promotions Office meeting, the team of five decided to hold the first meeting after a pizza and beer dinner at Tony's Pizza Plaza. Larry of Operations, Barry Moss of Finance, Steen Geertsen of HR, John Convery of Engineering, and Janet Kass from Marketing constituted the team. Tony's was crowded that night. There was a large table next to theirs where a girls' youth soccer team was having their season's awards ceremony. Theirs was a happy noisy group but the LPO folks were still able to converse.

After the pizza and two rounds of beer, Janet was first to speak. "Listen guys, I'm actually indifferent as to whether our products are made here or in China. Of course it would sadden me to see our plant shut down but we're getting hammered by competition. As for Lean, I was impressed that you were able to reduce the time it took to make our product in the factory from nineteen days to three days. But I have the same problems as Brady with the operation. The lead times are terrible. Okay, it's terrific that the time it takes for a piece of raw material entering the factory till it gets shipped as a finished product is only three day. But my issue is that the time it takes from a customer calling in an order until it is shipped is now averaging over seventy days. My competitor is doing it in forty-five days. If we can use Lean to get better than forty-five days, I'm all for it."

The four men were silent. They were shocked that it was taking more than seventy days to get an order through. Larry then asked, "Tell me, Janet, what could be an ambitious goal for us to reduce our lead time down to? What number of days would make our customers happy and make our competitors fear us?"

"Fifteen days!" Janet instantly replied. "If we had a fifteen-day lead time we would kill the competition."

Barry from Finance stood up from the table to speak. "I'll tell you guys something. It was I who encouraged Brady to look at sources in Asia. Competition has become tough and we no longer enjoy the same margins we had five years ago. Our costs are going up and the market won't allow us to raise prices. Most of our competitors are having their speakers made in China. I don't think we have much of a choice. On the other hand, there's another way to look at this. Right now when we order raw material, we have to pay for it thirty days after receipt. While that inventory is sitting in the raw material warehouse, it's useless to us. Thirty days after our customer receives our finished product they pay us. That means that there's a period that the inventory is costing us money. Right now I have to borrow the money from the bank to cover that period of time. If we could hit Amy's goal and achieve a fifteen-day lead time we would have positive cash flow and maybe justify keeping most of our production here and not need China.

"When you go to McDonald's to get a burger, you place your order, pay for it, they make it, and two minutes later you have it. They get their money before they pay for the raw materials. When our customers place an order, we can't deliver it in two minutes. We deliver it in seventy-five days."

Larry was thinking how happy he was to finally see all his peers focused on bringing Lean into the company. He spoke up. "I can see how we can all work together to take the waste out of our transactional processes. But there's an area where engineering can be a tremendous help and that's with *standardization*. So many of our products are so similar that from across a room they look identical. Also, some of the components we use are almost identical. Last time I counted, we had eighty-five different kinds of fasteners. If we could use more common parts for our products to share, we would help our costs as well as our lead times."

John spoke up. "While I certainly agree with your intention, that will be a hard sell with my engineers. They hate standardization. They like to start each design with a blank page and ignore any parts we already have in our existing directory. But I've been lax in that area and I will pledge to this group that I will kick off a real standardization program."

Barry ordered another round of beer from Tony and then turned to address the group. "They say that finance people are the only type of people who don't mind bayoneting the wounded. I'm the one that put the China bug in Brady's ear. I'm guilty as charged but I think that if we could paint a picture for him of a company with fifteen-day lead times, which incidentally would be the best in the industry, and positive cash flow, I think I could get him very excited about this Lean business."

Steen Geertsen from HR spoke. "It's clear we need to have a Kaizen event to reduce the order fulfillment cycle. The seventy-day order fulfillment cycle involves people in purchasing, planning, sales, receiving, shipping, and production. I'm positive that no one person in this company knows the entire process end-to-end. Everyone knows what happens in his or her own departments but nobody knows what happens in the adjacent departments. I think the first official task of our LPO is to conduct a Kaizen Event with the target of reducing our lead time to fifteen days.

"We have to construct a team with about eight people and send them an invitation letter. Each of your departments have to participate so I need each of you to give me the name or names of the people you want to participate in the event and I'll send out the letter.

"I think we're about to kick off something that will revolutionize our company."

*You can't plow a field
by turning it over in your mind.*

Irish Proverb

Discussion

From a Lean management standpoint:
What's going on in this chapter?

The leadership team has discovered that the customer is king. When this company started out, they had a hit product on their hands. It had become a cult loudspeaker and was very popular with college kids. They would rather have a defective pair of Sonic speakers than no Sonic speakers at all.

If the local shop was out of stock, they would happily wait another few weeks until they could have theirs. But manufacturing consumer products is a Darwinian game. Competition develops similar or better products. Competition offers better delivery times, like in the preceding chapter.

There's an old joke that illustrates this:

The United States Navy's Seventh Fleet was steaming into a harbor on a very foggy evening. The Admiral of the fleet was on the bridge of the flagship. It was the Admiral who first noticed the light ahead. The Admiral said to the signalman on the bridge with him, "flash a signal to that ship ahead and tell him to bear five degrees East." The young sailor dutifully manned his flashing signal light and sent out a Morse series of flashes. A few minutes passed before an answering series of flashing dots and dashes were seen. "What did he reply?" asked the Admiral. The sailor was writing down the reply on a pad. He said, "They want you to bear five degrees West."

"That's ridiculous," replied the Admiral. "They don't know who we are. Send another signal but this time say that we are the Seventh Fleet of the United States Navy and they must bear five degrees East." That signal was flashed out from the flagship's bridge. A few minutes later they received the reply flashes. "What are they saying now?" asked the Admiral.

The sailor replied, "They said you are to bear five degrees West." Now the Admiral was outraged. "Okay, send them this signal, 'I am an Admiral on board the flagship of the Seventh Fleet of the United States Navy and you had damn well bear five degrees East'." That signal was sent out and a few minutes later a return signal was received. "Now what is he saying?" asked the exasperated Admiral.

"He said that he is a Seaman First Class on a lighthouse and you had better bear five degrees West."

The point of this story is that, just as the Admiral couldn't move the lighthouse, a company can no longer push around their customers. Sonic has a seventy-day order fulfillment cycle and their competitor can do it in forty-five days. Sonic will lose their customers unless they improve their processes. It's as simple as that.

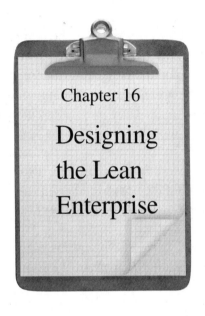

Chapter 16

Designing the Lean Enterprise

The next morning, eight people received this memo:

To: Kaizen Team Member
From: The Lean Promotions Office

You have been selected to participate in a Kaizen Event scheduled to take place next week. Because of your in-depth knowledge of the workings of your department, you will be a member of an 8-person team organized to improve one of our company's key processes. The event will begin at 8:00 a.m. Monday and will be completed at 4:30 Friday afternoon. This will be a full-time effort so we need you to clear your calendar for that week. You will not have time to attend any meetings or to even visit your department.

The recipients of the memo each asked their managers for an explanation of the memo but one of the secrets to the success of Kaizen events is the creation of a crisis. A crisis atmosphere is created when a team attends a Monday morning meeting and is told that they have to reduce the company's lead time from seventy days down to fifteen by Friday. The challenge seems impossible and the crisis atmosphere is created. A crisis sharpens the mind and demands teamwork. It was important not to let the team know what the challenge would be until that Monday morning.

The eight people were relieved of their responsibilities for a week and showed up the next Monday morning in the conference room without a clue as to what they were about to do.

Coffee and donuts were set out and the eight-person Kaizen Team took seats facing the front of the room where the five members of the LPO were sitting. Janet Kass from marketing addressed the Kaizen team.

"I want to welcome the eight of you to our Kaizen Event. First of all I need to make it clear that this isn't some sort of punishment. Each of you should be honored that you were chosen to be on this team. You were picked because you are considered an expert in your area.

"You are going to work this week on an important project because our company can no longer do business as we have in the past. Our competition is hurting us and if we don't change the way we do business, this operation will probably shut down. We have to change and I mean we have to change fast. Every one in this company will have to change the way they do their jobs or none of us will have jobs. It's as simple as that.

"Our executive team here—we call ourselves the Lean Promotions Office—has a challenge for you. Our current order fulfillment time is averaging seventy days. That's seventy days from the time the customer places the order until it gets shipped. Our competition is doing it in forty-five days. Your challenge is, by this Friday, to come up with a way to reduce our time down to fifteen days. It will not only make us a better supplier to our customers, it will tremendously improve our cash flow.

"Steen and Larry will lead you through the Kaizen Event this week. We will all get together again Friday afternoon at which time the eight of you will make a formal presentation to our LPO on how you got the lead time down to 15 days. I wish you good luck."

The eight team members were stunned. One of them spoke up. "Janet are you nuts? Giving us five days to come up with a method to reduce our lead times by 80 percent is like asking us to cure world hunger. Our order fulfillment process involves every department in this company. It even includes our suppliers."

The other stunned team members nodded in agreement. Janet replied, "I know this sounds like *mission impossible* but this Kaizen process is a powerful tool you're about to learn and both Steen and Larry have had some very good successes with it. You're in their capable hands and I think you will have a good time this week and come up with something you're going to be very proud of."

With that, John, Barry, and Janet left the room and turned the meeting over to Steen and Larry to conduct the Kaizen event.

Larry told the group that they would spend most of that day learning about Kaizen. Starting Monday afternoon they would study the existing process and then spend all day Wednesday and Thursday designing the new process. Friday morning would be used to prepare a PowerPoint presentation for the executives, and on Friday afternoon they would make the presentation.

Larry then showed the team a PowerPoint that one of his factory Kaizen teams had prepared for one of their projects. Then Steen showed them the results of the Kaizen events he led in HR. Viewing the PowerPoints allowed the team to see the application of the Kaizen tools: the MUDA hunt, the Red Tag Campaign, and flow charting.

Larry spent the remainder of the morning explaining the foundation of Kaizen. He spent quite a bit of time on what's called The Three Super Ordinate Principles of Kaizen.

Larry wrote the three principles on the flip chart.

- Better results come from process improvement

- Total Process Thinking

- Nonjudgmental environment

He then began his explanation. "The first Super Ordinate Principal means that, to get better results, you need to improve your process. In other words, you can't get better results simply by exhortation. Hanging posters that say 'We can do better' or setting tough goals won't bring about improved results. Better results are achieved by improving your process. And improving your process is achieved by discovering the waste in the process and permanently removing that waste. In Deming's fourteen points*, point number ten reads *'Eliminate slogans, exhortations, and targets for the work force asking for zero defects and new levels of productivity. Such exhortations only create adversarial relationships, as the bulk of the causes of low quality and low productivity belong to the system and thus lie beyond the power of the work force.'*

"The second principle, 'Total Process Thinking,' means that a company has to be run like a total system—not a bunch of fragments. Peter Drucker, in his book *Management,* says running a company is like leading a symphony orchestra. All the instruments have to play together if the music is to sound good. The trumpet player can't decide to play Dixieland while the rest of the orchestra is playing Mozart. But many leaders of companies don't understand that and set companies up as a series of competitors. First shift against second shift. Product A profits against Product B profits. People in those kinds of companies start hating each other because of the competitive atmosphere. They don't realize that 'The enemy is out there— not in our organization.'

"In Deming's fourteen points, point number nine reads *'Break down barriers between departments. People in research, design, sales, and production must work as a team, to foresee problems of production and in use that may be encountered with the product or service.'*

The third principle, 'Nonjudgmental Environment' is probably the most important of the three. In a company where there is a high degree of judgmentalism, there is usually a high degree

Read about Deming *and* Deming's Fourteen Points *in the* Appendix

of fear. In Deming's fourteen points, point number 8 reads, *'Drive out fear, so that everyone may work effectively for the company.'* In companies where there is a high degree of judgmentalism you usually find an aversion to risk taking because people are fearful of being criticized for making bad decisions. Process improvement is rare in those companies.

"Companies suffering from judgmentalism are ones where the focus is on WHO screwed up instead of WHAT IS screwed up. In those companies we find problems being covered up for years sometimes with finger pointing and lying."

Larry then covered other aspects of the foundation of Kaizen that included:

- The importance of standardization

- The importance of housekeeping

- The elimination of MUDA (waste)

He had several videos explaining these aspects of Lean that the company purchased online.

By mid-afternoon they were ready to start charting the order fulfillment process using sticky notes spread across four flip chart pages.

Hannah Bley from sales volunteered to put up the sticky notes since the total fulfillment process started at the sales desk in her department.

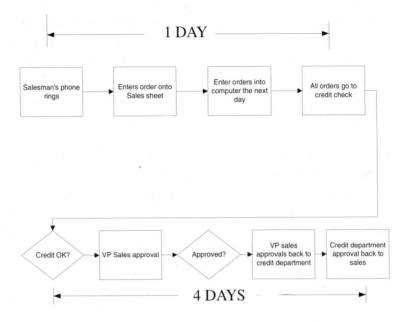

In just a few minutes, she posted these nine sticky notes and turned to explain.

"I know you're going to think this is crazy, but it's the way our sales department operates today. Our salesmen are all very busy and even though we have a computerized order entry system, they still find it easier to write the order down on a sales sheet. They typically wait until the morning of the next day to enter the orders into the system. If one is out sick the next day, his orders wait.

"We have a rule that all orders have to go through credit check. We need to be sure that the customer isn't on credit hold or that he's not going over the credit limit. If they approve the customer's credit, they put a rubber date stamp onto the sales order and sign it. If the order is exceptional, the sales order sheet has to go to the VP of Sales. If he approves it, he also rubber stamps it and signs the sheet. His signed sheets then go back to the sales department who then pass it back to the salesman. This process typically takes five days but if any one of the people in the chain is out sick, all the orders in their batch wait an additional day. I would guess that the average turn around time is seven working days."

Larry got up to take a close look at the sticky notes. He turned to face the group. "Before we add any more sticky notes, let's talk about what is going on. It looks like all the processing is taking place in batches. Instead of the salesman putting the order online immediately and getting the credit check started, all the orders wait a full day. If he's out sick the next day, the orders wait two days. It's the same thing for the credit checks. They too are passed on to the VP of Sales in batches.

"Why don't we pause in our process diagramming and have a MUDA hunt. I would like the eight of you to take twenty minutes and see how many forms of MUDA we have right here. Remember to list all your MUDA observations in the form of a question. We're not judgmental here."

Muda Hunt Results

Muda of Overproduction

- Why does the salesman make a "batch" of orders of his sales sheets to give to the credit department?
- Why does the credit department make a batch of credit checks to give to the VP of sales?
- Why does the VP of sales make a batch of credit approvals to give to the sales department?

Muda of Inventory

- Why is there such a large backlog of orders between the sales department and credit?
- Why is there so much paperwork?

Muda of Conveyance

- Why are there 4 handoffs?
- Why does paperwork have to be distributed?

Muda of Motion

- Why do salesmen bother with manual sales sheets?
- Why does the sales department bother with manual sales sheets?
- Why does the VP of sales bother with manual sales order sheets?
- Why all the rubber stamps and manual signatures?

000

Muda of Processing

- Why do all orders have to go through credit check?

- Why does the VP of Sales have to send the sheets back to the credit department and not to the salesman?

Muda of Waiting

- Why do orders have to wait a full day with the salesmen?

- Why do orders have to wait a full day in the credit department?

- Why do orders have to wait a full day with the VP of sales?

- Why do orders approved by the VP of Sales have to wait a full day before getting processed?

- Why do we run out of parts so frequently?

Larry had the team write their MUDA HUNT results on a flip-chart page for review by the group. He then asked, "This process is now taking five days. Can we come up with a way to cut it down to just one day?"

Hannah spoke up. "I've worked in the sales department now for three years and I never understood why we do things the way we do. I've tried to make suggestions before, but nobody seems to be interested in my ideas. First of all, I think it's ridiculous for the salesmen to use the handwritten sales sheets. They tell me they're very busy and it's easier to fill in the sales sheet than to enter the orders into the computer. They're just making extra work for themselves. We have the system online, but we keep using a manual system from the old days. If we did nothing more than have the salesmen enter the orders online and send them on to credit check, we could cut one full day off our total cycle time."

One of the team members, Brett Bannerman, was from the IS department. He spoke up. "This MUDA hunt gave me some ideas. What we have is a sort of *batch and queue system*. We want to have more of a *one-piece flow system*. With today's system, if a customer is the first of fifty customers to call in an order in a day, he will become the fiftieth person in line because his order won't move until all the orders for that day get processed the next day. I'm pretty sure that, with very little effort, we can cut the five days to less than one day."

He went to the front of the room and started writing notes that he put on the board.

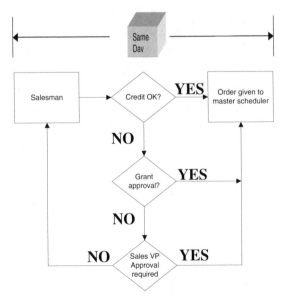

He then explained. "Here's how we can cut the cycle down to one day. First, we need to get rid of the paperwork and that won't be hard. We can require that the salesman enter each order into the system as he receives it. If it's an existing customer calling, our system can give the salesman instant credit information. Let's say we give the salesmen authorization to approve all orders that fall within the customer's approved amount and that the customer isn't on credit hold. If that's the case, he just checks off a box marked 'approved' and the order goes to master scheduling in the factory. It would be an almost instantaneous transaction.

"Let's say the order is over the customer's credit limit. In that case, the salesman would check a box marked 'credit check required'. Those orders would electronically get sent to the credit department. If the credit checks out, we could set up an electronic signature system so that the credit people could approve the order and electronically sign their approval.

"In those cases where the customer is way over their credit limit or there's some issue requiring executive approval, the credit department would check the box marked 'VP Approval Required'. Those orders would be sent to the VP. If he approves it, he would electronically sign it and the message would get sent to master scheduling, the credit departments, and the salesman.

"What I just described would take very little programming time but let me write on this flow chart what it would eliminate."

- No more batching of orders. They would be processed as they came in.

- No more papers to transport, handle, stamp, and sign.

- Salesmen would no longer have to wait for the credit department to pass on the VP's approval.

- Since we would no longer be processing in batches, if somebody were out for a day, a whole batch of orders wouldn't be delayed.

The team agreed that the proposal was good and that, with less than an hour of working together, they cut about a week out of the order fulfillment cycle. Larry then had Hannah and Brett sit down and asked who would like to continue adding sticky notes to the flow.

The next person to start writing sticky notes was Jeff Trester, the company's master scheduler. "Since I'm the next person in the chain, I should best be able to describe what happens next." He put up these sticky notes.

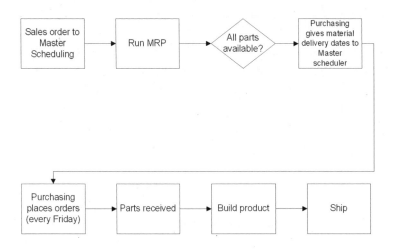

Jeff turned to face the team. "I know this looks like a straight forward process but it's not. The steps I've shown here take a total of sixty-six days."

A team members spoke up, "Sorry to interrupt you Jeff but I don't understand your first box. What does Run MRP mean?"

Jeff replied, "Sorry for the jargon. MRP* stands for Material Resource Planning. It's a computer program we use to determine material purchase requirements—when and how much—based on lead times and quantity discounts. We tell the computer what products we want to build in the next ninety days and the computer tells us if we have the materials on hand and if not, how much we need to buy. Unfortunately, it takes many hours to run the MRP program so we only run it on weekends. If I get an order from sales on Monday, it has to sit until the next Monday—after the MRP run. But it occurred to me that running our MRP program only on weekends probably isn't necessary. We got a new, faster MRP program last year that we still only run on weekends. I'm pretty sure we can run it overnight twice a week from now on.

"But the MRP report doesn't know when the material will arrive. Purchasing needs to call the suppliers to get that information. Unfortunately, I have to wait a full day for that information because purchasing gives it to me in one batch and it takes them a day to accumulate all that information. Once I know the dates the materials will arrive here, I can tell the sales department when we can build the product. But there's another source of delay there. The purchasing department only orders materials on Friday. Purchase orders going to the purchasing department on Monday will sit there until Friday.

See explanation of MRP in the Appendix.

"Let's say that the sales department gives me their orders on Monday. Those sit until the following Monday. And let's say the parts we need for that order aren't in house. If the purchasing department gets those orders on Monday, they will wait until Friday. The longest time element in this process is in getting the parts here from Asia. It takes the vendor thirty days to make the parts there and then it takes eighteen days to get here by ship." Jeff then added two boxes with arrows to his diagram. "This process can take as long as sixty-six days assuming the orders wait five days for MRP and then wait another four days for purchasing to place the orders.

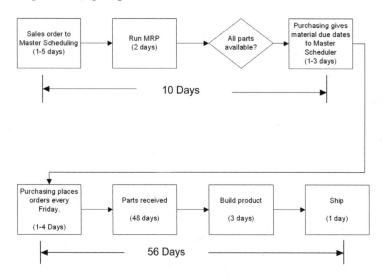

"If we add these sixty-six days to the five days it takes to get the order to master scheduling, we're looking at about a seventy-day cycle. I know our competition is doing it in forty-five days, but I don't see how we can cut it down to fifteen days."

Larry then offered, "You all know the next step. We need to find the waste in this process. Let's take twenty minutes once again and do a MUDA hunt."

Muda Hunt Results

Muda of Overproduction

- Why does purchasing give the sales department material due dates in a batch?
- Why does purchasing only order every Friday with a batch of purchase orders?

Muda of Inventory

- Why is there such a large backlog of purchase orders?
- Why do we need so many different parts to build our products?
- Why are there so many parts waiting for incoming inspection?

Muda of Processing

- Why do we need to place purchase orders in order to get parts?
- Why do we do incoming inspection?

Muda of Waiting

- Why does purchasing wait a day before telling sales when material will be available?
- Why do so many of our product builds have to wait 48 days for shipping parts from Asia?
- Why does purchasing place orders only on Fridays?
- Why do we run out of parts in the warehouse?

The team silently studied the process map they had created. Steen Geertsen had been quiet up until this point. He walked over to the pile of blank sticky notes, started filling some out and as he began sticking them onto the wall he explained. "I've spent my whole career in HR and this is my first exposure to what happens in operations. I'm going to try to make a new process with these sticky notes that shows an order fulfillment process with all our MUDA removed."

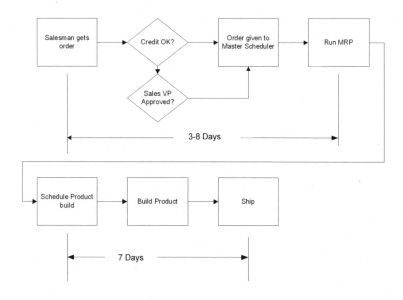

"Excuse me mister HR," one of the team members said. "You showed us how to cut our time down to fifteen days but didn't you leave out an important detail? You left out the forty-eight days it takes our parts to get here from Asia."

"I know that," Steen replied. "But it seems that if we happen to have all the parts we need in stock, we really could ship our products fifteen days after the customer ordered it."

Jeff Trester, the master scheduler stood up and angrily shot back at Steen, "And if I had wheels, I'd be a school bus! We hardly ever have all the parts we need. We use over 10,000 different parts to build out products. We would need a warehouse the size of Europe to store every single part we need. Why don't you stick to HR process improvements?"

"Hold on a minute you two," interjected Larry. "I think Steen is on to something here. As you all know, we build our products according to a sales forecast. As far as I know, there are only two kinds of forecasts—lucky and lousy. Because of our poor forecasting, our warehouse is full of product our customers don't want and we are constantly expediting parts to build the products we should have in the warehouse but don't.

"What if the factory could build any product the customer wanted in ten seconds? I'll tell you what that would mean. It would mean we wouldn't need a warehouse for finished goods. We would stop being a 'make to forecast' company and become a 'make to order' company. Of course we will never make our products in ten seconds but the quicker we can react, the easier it will be to become a 'make to order' company. Isn't that the business model Dell Computers uses?

"It seems to me that we make two kinds of products here: products we sell in high volume but make a small margin, and products we sell in low quantities that we make a high margin on. Maybe we have no business making the high volume low margin products here. Maybe those products should be made in Asia. Maybe we should stop selling some of those products.

"Half our company's profits come from the high margin products. Perhaps we should keep product development here and only manufacture our high end products in our own factory. I think we can come up with a fulfillment process for those products where the lead time will be fifteen days.

"One of my concerns with moving our production to Asia is what it would do to our workforce. We have people who have been with the company for over twenty years. I think we could outsource our low-end products to Asia and keep all our employees. Marketing tells me they could sell more of the high end product if we could improve our lead times and reduce our costs. We now have an opportunity to all work together and make that happen.

"I think we have about two dozen high end products. They fall into three families of design. We could form a team with members from engineering, marketing, and our key suppliers to see how many opportunities there are to start using common parts in these models. I don't think we need to do any major re-designing. We could look at things like packaging and fasteners, for example. The fewer parts we use in our company, the easier it will be to assure that we have all the parts here that we need.

"A simple thing we can implement immediately is to say that all future new products will only use components from a selected list of what will become our 'common design elements.'

"The fifteen-day lead time, unfortunately, is going to be a long-term project. Let's see what we can do right away to reduce the lead times. I'll give you twenty minutes to review the MUDA hunt list and make a list of recommendations for an improved fulfillment process."

The team produced this list:

- Purchasing should discontinue the practice of ordering materials only on Friday.

- Purchasing should report the material delivery dates as soon as they get them and not wait until they have a batch of dates to report.

- We shouldn't have to inspect every part that is delivered. We should have suppliers who do the inspection before it leaves their facility. That could cut a day from our cycle.

- We shouldn't need to issue purchase orders for every part. A simple Kanban system could alert our suppliers when a re-order point has been reached.*

Larry made a flow chart using sticky notes. If we removed this MUDA, we could cut six days off our cycle time. There's nothing stopping us from immediately implementing these improvements. Cutting the lead time down to fifty-five days is quite an achievement but we know it's possible to cut it down to fifteen days and that must become our goal."

* *See Appendix for explanation of* Kanban

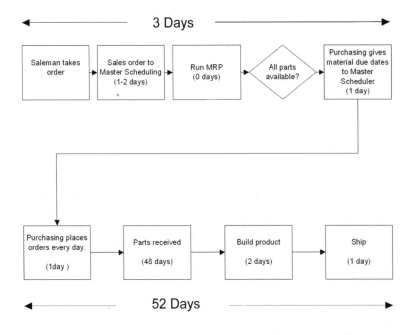

Larry turned to Barry Moss, the head of finance. "Tell me something, Barry," he asked, "How can we calculate how much money we would save by cutting our lead time down to fifteen days?"

Barry scratched his head and just stared at Larry without saying a word. Then his eyes widened as the answer came to him. He walked up to the flip chart and, before writing anything, turned to speak. "The biggest benefit, of course, to reducing our lead times is that we will be able to hold onto our customers and attract new ones. I'm not sure how to put that in terms of dollars saved. But there's no question that reducing our lead times will reduce the number of days that we must hold onto our inventories of finished goods as well as raw materials."

181

He then did the following calculation on the flip chart.

Cost of Good Sold

$30 million is sales/year x 50% cost of goods sold = $15 million total cost of goods sold.

Inventory on hand based upon current 10 day lead time.

10 days lead time / 365 days per year x $15 million cost of goods sold = $2,876,712 current inventory value.
(Inventory turns = 365 days per year / 10 day lead time = 5.2 turns)

Projected inventory on hand based upon 15 day lead time.

15 days lead time /365 days per year x $15 million cost of goods sold = $616,431.
(Inventory turns = 365 days per year/15 days lead time = 24.3)

Inventory Reduction

$2,876712 - $616,431= $2,260,215
(Inventory turn improvement = 24.3 - 5.2 = 19.1 turns)

Savings

12% Inventory carrying cost x $2,260,215= $271,233.

Larry stood up to look at the flip chart and then turned to the group. "This is fantastic. We had three little Kaizen events and already we can show about $300,000 in annual savings. It's not going to be too hard to beat Brady's 20 percent China savings.

It is not who is right,
but what is right, that is of importance.

Thomas Hardey

Chapter 17

2-Day
Lead Time

Larry took the team out for lunch. They needed a break from the conference room. Larry watched his team devour their burgers and engage in animated discussions about the project. He was thrilled with the degree to which the team had become engaged in this project.

After lunch Larry saw that the restaurant had pretty much emptied out and suggested that they continue the discussion in the quiet restaurant before returning to the conference room.

"I think we have two separate problems to solve," Larry began. "I don't see why we couldn't maintain a stock of the raw material we need for our popular products. If we always had stock on hand to produce our key models, then Steen's depiction of the fifteen-day cycle would be a reality. We could increase our investment in raw material. I'd rather invest in raw material than in finished goods. Investing in finished goods is what we're doing today and we have a finished goods warehouse full of product nobody wants and we constantly run out of finished goods we need.

"Even if we doubled our inventory of raw materials, the net investment wouldn't be much if we focused on raw material for our popular models. That's how we would handle our high-margin low-volume products. I don't think we have any business manufacturing our high-volume low-margin products. Those really could come from Asia.

"I think we could get a supplier in Asia to build those high-volume products there and hold a twenty-one-day supply in their inventory. We would agree to hold an additional twenty-one-day supply here. In that way, when we deplete our inventory, the supplier would immediately ship his twenty-one-day supply here. It would take eighteen days to get here and say another three days to get through our receiving process.

"So when we've fully implemented this plan, we would say most of our models made in this factory would have a fifteen-day lead time. The fringe models, of course, would have a fifty-six-day lead time because we wouldn't necessarily maintain all the parts for them in stock.

"I think we're just about ready to make a presentation to our Lean Promotions Office team and tell them how we can quickly reduce our lead times from seventy-one days down to fifteen. I think the really exciting news is that our plan to maintain twenty-one days of inventory of the high-volume finished products made in Asia would have a two-day lead time since we won't be building any ourselves and we should never run out of inventory."

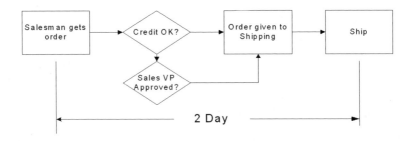

> *Do more than exist, live.*
> *Do more than touch, feel.*
> *Do more than read, absorb.*
> *Do more than hear, listen.*
> *Do more than think, ponder.*
> *Do more than talk, say something.*
>
> **John H. Rhodes**

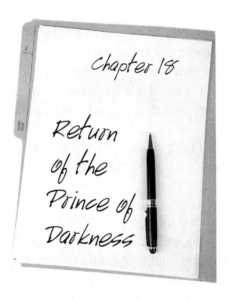

Chapter 18

Return of the Prince of Darkness

Larry was in a great mood enjoying his drive in to work along the pretty country roads, watching the sunrise, and listening to his favorite radio station. As soon as he pulled into the company parking lot, he spotted Jim Brady's BMW parked in his reserved spot near the front entrance. Brady had been on a trip to China and had been out of the office for two weeks. Two glorious weeks!

The office was so much more pleasant when Brady wasn't there. The joke had always been that Brady had a way of lighting up a room when he left it. He seemed to have a perpetual scowl and would often walk by people in hallways without even acknowledging them. He was not what you call a "people person."

Larry walked into the building and went right to the coffee pot in the hallway to pour himself a cup. Jim Brady's secretary, Linda, was there having just filled her cup. "Good morning, Larry," she said after taking her first sip of her almost overfilled cup. "I guess you see that Jim is back from China. I don't ever remember seeing him so happy. He's very excited about what he saw there. He wanted me to get the staff together for a 10:00 meeting so he can tell you all about his trip."

"Okay, Linda, I'll be there at 10:00." Larry walked down the hall to his office irritated because his great mood had been destroyed.

Jim Brady's staff assembled in his office at 10:00 and were surprised to see a happy Jim Brady. He had just returned from China the night before but wasn't showing any signs of jetlag. As a matter of fact he seemed unusually energized and looked like he was ready to burst out with some sort of earth-shaking announcement.

Brady leaned way back in his chair, put his two hands behind his neck, broke out in a big smile, and began. "I've been on a trip these past two weeks that will change our lives. Even though before leaving on the trip I had seen websites and brochures of the companies I was about to visit, I really didn't expect to see just how terrific these places were. China is no longer a country that produces nothing but cheap knockoffs. These facilities are as sophisticated as anything we have in America. I visited companies there making high definition television displays, third generation cell phones, and computer and networking hardware. They not only manufacture products for top American companies, they now do their own product development. I learned that there's not a single hour of engineering invested in these products by Palm, Sony, Ericson, and others. All they do is put their names on these entry-level products and engineer only the more advanced models themselves.

"We have no choice. It doesn't make sense not to outsource. I'm convinced that we can get a 20 percent savings by having our products made in China. Right now our competitors are outsourcing and, as a result, they are underpricing us in the marketplace and we are losing market share.

"By outsourcing we will not only reduce our costs, we will be reducing our capital spending. We will no longer need capital— our supplier in China will have all the machines we need. By divesting ourselves of manufacturing, we can go from fixed cost to variable cost. In other words, *we will only pay for what we sell.* How cool will that be?

"The logic is simple. For some of our products, materials represent as much as 80 percent of the cost to manufacture. These Chinese factories not only have low labor rates since they typically pay their workers less than ninety cents an hour, they keep their material costs down because of their sheer buying power. One company I visited manufactures nothing but loudspeakers. They aggregate the demand from their dozens of loudspeaker customers and use that clout in the marketplace to get better prices and a more stable supply of parts than any American manufacturer of loudspeakers could muster on its own.

"My vision is to become very profitable by jumping on the

same outsourcing bandwagon that companies all over America are jumping on. We could shrink this organization down to a small efficient team. I could eliminate most of the engineers as well as all the departments that support the factory since the factory will be gone. Not only will I get my products made cheaper, I won't have all the overhead expenses I'm now saddled with. We could then move into a much smaller building, and not have to deal with all the problems of having a factory. I'm sick of the ridiculous increases in our costs of energy to run the place; our health insurance premiums are obscene; I'm spending a fortune on litigation; this city's regulations are unrealistic; the anti-pollution laws are ridiculously restrictive; our workforce is ageing; I can't get help that can read or speak English; and I don't want to schedule any more government mandated sexual harassment training. I've had it!

"I want to move ahead on this plan and I'm counting on each of you to help me do it as quickly as possible. My goal is to have all of our products made in China. I want production to start there within four months."

At that point, Linda opened the door to Brady's office and stuck her head in. "Jim, I thought you would want to know, Mike Bartlett is on the phone. Should I tell him you'll call him back?"

"No, put him on hold—I need to talk to him." Brady stood up as if to give a signal that the meeting had just ended. "Okay, team, I'm sorry I don't have time to discuss this further at this point. Bartlett, our outsourcing consultant whom I traveled to China with is on the phone and we have a lot to talk about. I need each of you to start thinking about a transition plan and who is going to have to do what." Brady didn't wait until his staff had filed out of the office when he picked up his phone. They all heard him say into the phone, "Mike baby how's the jetlag and the hangover this morning?"

The staff was stunned as they filed into Larry Smith's office. Janet was first to speak. "I think Jim has lost his mind. I wonder what kind of Kool Aid they gave him to drink over there? I don't think he has thought this whole thing through. I'm sure there's some logic to us doing some outsourcing, but to just shut everything down here is nuts."

Larry then spoke, "This is my fourth year here and it's an okay place to work, but there are people in the plant who have been here for more than twenty years. They have spent more time with people they work with in the plant than they spent with their children during the years the children lived at home. Also this isn't a very big city and we are a pretty big employer. This is going to hurt the community.

"If we shut down the factory, I won't have a job and neither will the people who work for and depend on me. I'm not going down without a fight. We really need to think about how to deal with Mr. Brady.

"I've told you that I had a feeling as if the clock to the time bomb is ticking. Now I know when the bomb goes off—four months from now."

The staff returned to their own offices but none of them got much work done that day.

God grant me patience.
And I want it now.

Anon

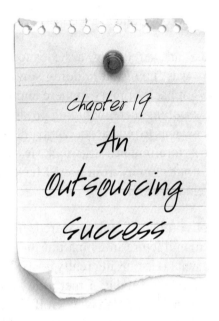

Chapter 19

An

Outsourcing

Success

Larry didn't have much of an appetite for dinner that evening. After dinner he looked out the front window and saw his neighbor, Bob, washing his car. Larry walked across the street while watching Bob run the soapy rag across a fender. "You sure look like you like that car a lot, Bob"

"Are you kidding, Larry?" Bob looked up smiling. "I love this car."

"Bob, let me help you wash the car and then maybe you could take a few minutes and listen to my latest problem at work."

"Sure thing," Bob replied. "I would appreciate the company."

After washing the beautiful Corvette and putting it away in the garage, they went into the house, grabbed two Pacificos from the refrigerator, and went into Bob's office.

"Okay, what's on your mind?" asked Bob.

"This is serious," answered Larry as he leaned forward. "I told you that Brady was interested in doing some outsourcing to Asia. Well, he got back from a trip there and is now planning to outsource everything there including product development. It sounds like he wants to reduce our company into an operation that can fit into a storefront in a strip mall. He's even announced a target date—four months from now. I have four months to create a Lean enterprise."

"That is a serious problem," Bob answered. "People are fleeing our shores to manufacture in China but the truth is that few people realize what outsourcing really costs. Let me give you an example I just heard today. I met a guy who told me he recently purchased a set of Callaway Golf clubs and a bag for $250. That's a bargain because the bag alone goes for over $400.

"There was a problem, and he sent them back to Callaway for repair. Callaway, of course wouldn't touch it. It was a Chinese knockoff. They copied every detail right down to the patent numbers. The Callaway people gave this guy a copy of a press release that described how Callaway had pursued enforcement actions in eleven countries involving 37,000 individual counterfeited products including Callaway golf clubs, bags, and clothing.

"That was the kind of problem that concerned my company,

Apache Cycle Components, two years ago when we looked into outsourcings our bicycle component manufacturing to China. Some of our high-end components are manufactured with proprietary processes we developed and perfected over the years. They are our company secrets—one of our 'core competencies'*. If we had those products made in China, we would have to give them our secret processes and we were concerned that they would then come out with their own brand of product using this same manufacturing process. Control of intellectual property in China, unfortunately, isn't very strong.

"But our competition was outsourcing and taking market share on some of our models. We were very concerned about what outsourcing could do to our employees and to the community. As it turned out, we eventually did quite a bit of outsourcing to China but that hasn't reduced our headcount very much.

"Our company makes some very expensive components. These are manufactured using our proprietary manufacturing processes. There were two reasons we wouldn't consider outsourcing these. First is the issue of our secret processes and second is that the volume isn't very much and the demand for our high-end models is unpredictable.

"Every year we develop more of these high-end products. We call them our 'flagship products.' Once these models mature, we then develop a low-end version of them that sells for about 80 percent less than the flagship. The flagship models are sold in fancy bike shops and the low-end models are sold in stores

* See explanation of core competency in the discussion section at the end of this chapter.

like Wal-Mart. Of course, the low end products aren't manufactured with our proprietary machining processes; they are mostly stamped.

"Our strategy was to outsource the low-end products but keep the high-end stuff here. By doing this, our development engineers had a factory to make themselves prototypes and we had a factory that could respond very quickly to the unpredictable demand for the high end products.

"We were heavily into our Lean transformation at that time and we redesigned the fabrication and assembly areas that produced the high-end product. We created what's called a mixed model assembly line."

"Okay, Bob, hold it right there," Larry interrupted. "Explain what a mixed model assembly line is."

"A mixed model line is something Toyota came up with. They knew that they couldn't copy Ford's methods back in the 1930s. Ford had the luxury of high demand for each model. That allowed them to dedicate assembly lines, for example, to one particular model. Toyota developed clever assembly lines that would make all their models all the time. If you watched one of these Toyota mixed model assembly lines run, you would see big cars followed by small cars and then followed by big cars again. No dedicated lines, just highly flexible ones that had all the tools and all the parts to make many models at the same time.

"And that's what we did in our factory. And do you know what happened? Our cost dropped tremendously. They dropped for a funny reason. It wasn't just because of our new assembly lines. While developing the Chinese sources to manufacture our low-end products, we discovered fantastic sources in China for the components we need in the U.S. to build our high-end Apache products. We were able to reduce the cost of those components by 17 percent. Leaning out our fulfillment processes on these high-end products caused our lead times to drop from weeks to days. Then the greatest thing happened—our demand skyrocketed. We couldn't make the high-end products fast enough.

"It was during that time that we were transitioning our low-end products to be manufactured in China. It worked out really well for our factory folks because, as we needed fewer and fewer people to make the low-end products, we needed more and more to do the high-end. As it turned out, I think we lost about 15 percent of the factory workforce but we were carrying 15 percent temporary workers at that time, so no full-time people lost their jobs.

"It all worked out in the end, we kept our engineering staff and retained our proprietary processes but I'll tell you it wasn't simple to transition those low-end products to China. We had lots of bumps in the road and I don't think we wound up saving what we anticipated.

I hope this helps you Larry."

Larry drank down the last of his beer and answered, "It helps me a lot. I think we could come up with a similar strategy. I gotta go home, but I don't think I'll get much sleep tonight."

Success is not final. Failure is not fatal.
It is the courage to continue that counts.

Winston Churchill

Discussion

From a Lean management standpoint:
What's going on in this chapter?

Larry has a right to be upset. His boss, Jim Brady, thinks he found a shortcut to solving all his problems. Outsourcing to China is his key to success—his silver bullet.

The number of American companies that outsource to China is increasing by about 15 percent a year. Many of these companies view outsourcing as an opportunity to reduce costs and increase flexibility.

Many executives, however, fail to realize that outsourcing can be much more complicated and time-consuming than manufacturing in-house. While it may be easy to see that labor and material costs are cheaper in China, it is harder to pin down the costs of stolen intellectual property, complex supply chains, inflexible manufacturing schedules, more inventory, more write-offs, unanticipated air shipment expenses, the cost of laying off your U.S. people, and project management overhead. Many firms are unprepared for the amount of project management required, including late-night phone conferences, last minute travel for many staff members, and supply chain monitoring.

What to outsource and what to make in-house depends on the company's core competencies. A core competency is any activity or practice, such as product development, critical to a company's long-term success and growth. Typically, core competencies are based on skills or knowledge sets rather than products or functions. They provide maximum return on investment and act as barriers to other companies trying to enter the market.

Companies should not outsource if:

- Proprietary technology or proprietary manufacturing processes are involved. Anything that gives a company a unique advantage in the marketplace should not be outsourced. China and other Asian countries are popular outsourcing areas but intellectual property laws are not very strong there. Companies run a serious risk of losing their secrets.

- High-margin products are involved. A company should never outsource the products producing the greatest profits.

- Products require complex manufacturing or test processes.

- Products have low annual unit or dollar volume.

- Numerous engineering changes will occur during the first stages of production. A common way for Asian companies to gain more revenue from the American customer is through various ways of billing for engineering change orders.

It will be easier and easier for American firms to outsource to China just as they adjusted to Japan during the 1970s and 1980s. But right now the adjustment is still in the embryonic phase. An outsourcing study in 2005 by the firm Pittiglio Rabin Todd and McGrath found 65 percent of companies that outsource manufacturing offshore are satisfied with their relationship.

Yet only 4 percent of the 150 executives they surveyed were "very satisfied" with their offshore manufacturing relationship after less than one year. Even after five years, that figure barely doubled to 9 percent. Only after more than five years did the number of "very satisfied" customers rise to 23 percent.

It takes time and commitment to make Chinese manufacturing relationships work (as described in the skateboard manufacturer's story earlier in this book). In some cases the relationships don't work at all. As companies discover all the hidden costs of outsourcing, they may find that the 20 percent savings they anticipated didn't materialize.

There are advantages to keeping some production in America. Extended supply chains are slow to react to schedule changes. A producer in the United States can respond within 24 hours to changes in product mix, such as color, packaging, and delivery location. In China it takes five to six weeks. The same is true for response time for other unforeseen issues such as quality problems, supplier shortages, or inflexible lead times.

Beware of being in the thick of thin things.

C. Tovey

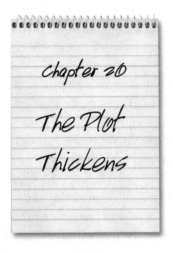

Chapter 20

The Plot Thickens

Larry didn't sleep well that night. It was 2:00 a.m. when his wife Sue woke up to see him next to her in bed reading a book. She asked him, "What are you doing reading a book? It's 2:00 o'clock in the morning!"

"I can't fall asleep. I'm really depressed about what's happening at work. I can't even believe it's really happening. I finally get to the point where I got all these improvements in place, I got all my peers excited about Lean, things are about to turn around and now I get the rug pulled out from under me by Brady and his hair-brained plan to shut the place down. You know what, Sue? Screw it; I'm putting my resume on Monster.com. I don't need this."

Sue let Larry rant and then offered, "Let me give you a good piece of advice, my dear. A really smart woman once told me, *'Ignore any thoughts that come to you in the middle of the night.'* Try to get some sleep and things will look a lot different in the morning."

Larry woke up and things did look different. He had a plan and was eager to get to work to put it into play.

He pulled into the parking lot and there was Brady's car. Not only did the sight of Brady make him angry, it had gotten to the point where the sight of Brady's car even upset him. As soon as he got into his office, he arranged for the staff to meet with him to put a plan into action.

The first one to speak at the meeting was Janet Kass. "I don't know about the rest of you guys, but I didn't get a very good night's sleep. I spent the night thinking about how to persuade Brady not to jump too quickly on this China thing. I would like us to try to persuade him to re-think this. I'm really good at preparing and presenting PowerPoints. We could make one that shows how we now have a Lean Promotions Office and how Lean will create a Lean Enterprise for us. We can show how much money we will save and how our lead times will improve. It could be an impressive presentation and...."

Barry Moss was scowling and interrupted Janet as soon as she paused to take a breath. "Janet that won't work. I've been Brady's CFO for ten years and I know how his brain works. A slick PowerPoint won't persuade him. First of all, his attention span is ridiculously short. And secondly, if he doesn't come up with the idea, he won't consider it a good idea. With Brady, you've got to shove a gold nugget under his nose and let him think he discovered it on his own.

"We need Brady to discover the improvements we've made with Lean and we need him to come up with the idea that it's dumb to outsource everything we make and shut down our factory. The question is; how do we pull that off?"

Larry replied, "I think it's up to each of us in the next few days to shove those gold nuggets under Brady's nose and hope he sees them."

Later that afternoon Jim Brady walked down the hall into the engineering department and stepped into John Convery's office. "John, we got a problem. I just had a meeting with our distributor and we've got to make the engineering change on the cabinet of the Radiance model. This has to happen fast and there can be no screw-ups. I need you to personally walk this one through. I think Angie is an idiot. I don't know why you don't fire her."

John was used to Brady's tirades. "Calm down, Jim. Did you forget that just a few weeks ago we invited you to see the results of the Kaizen event we conducted to improve the ECR process? Our new process is working great and I have no doubt that this ECR will go through quickly with no errors. Take a few minutes out. I want to show you something in the cafeteria."

Convery walked Brady to the cafeteria. It was break time for the factory and more than half the chairs were filled with production workers. They all looked up as the two executives walked through the door. Convery gave them all a big smile. Brady ignored them and just kept following Convery who was leading him to a large bulletin board on the wall.

"Jim, take a look at our new bulletin board. Your staff formed what we call the Lean Promotions Office and this bulletin board shows the results of all the activities we've been working on." The board had information about the Kaizen events for the ECR process, the HR Start Pack process and the lead time improvement project.

Convery showed Brady the one page three-part summary showing the trend and action items associated with the ECR project. He showed him the chart that projected the process would drop from sixteen days down to six within twenty weeks. But the report showed that the time had already gotten down to only four days and the project only started three weeks before.

Brady studied the chart and seemed a little impressed. But he didn't even look at any of the other charts and photos on the bulletin board.

"Okay, John, I suppose you have things under control." And with that Jim Brady returned to his office. John Convery grabbed a cup of coffee and sat at a table with three ladies from the coil-winding department for a nice chat.

After the break, John walked into Larry's office, shut the door and said, "I don't know what's wrong with Brady. He has no appreciation for what we're trying to accomplish and today he suggested I fire Angie. She doesn't deserve that kind of talk."

"You're right," Larry shot back. "Our job as leaders is not to inflict pain. Our job is to absorb pain. We need to keep Brady away from our people."

"But, Larry" Convery replied, "why on earth is he like that? You've been here a long time—has he always been like that?"

"I'll tell you why he's like that. Do you know the old story about the turtle and the scorpion? It goes like this:

"It seems that one day a scorpion and a turtle were standing on the bank of a flood-swollen river. Both needed to get across. Both were pondering their chances.

"The scorpion suggested to the turtle that he ride on the turtle's back across the river. 'From my perch, I could keep an eye out for logs and other debris that could smash into you...I'd be your early warning system.'

"'Yeah,' said the weary turtle, 'but you could also sting me to death.'

"'Well, that wouldn't make any sense,' replied the scorpion, 'it is in my self interest to keep you afloat.'

"The turtle considered that for a while, and then decided to carry the scorpion across. About mid-point in the river, however, the scorpion stung the turtle right in the back of the neck.

"In his dying gasp, the turtle asked, 'why?'

"'Hey,' said the scorpion, 'what can I tell you—it's my nature.'

"And that's Brady. It's his nature. I'm upset that he would suggest you fire Angie. He is so damned judgmental. That's one of the diseases of this company —judgmentalism. It creates fear and that creates an aversion to risk taking.

"He thinks that your clerk Angie is incompetent because of the performance of our ECR process. And he probably thinks Patty in the human resources department is sensational because we never hear about problems with any of the processes in that department.

"As you know, one of the three Super Ordinate Principles of Kaizen is to create a non-judgmental work environment. W. Edward Deming had strong feelings on that subject.

"In his book, *Out of the Crisis* he says, 'Fair rating is impossible. A common fallacy is the supposition that it is possible to rate people; to put them in rank order of performance for next year based upon performance last year.'

"He then goes on to illustrate this point with what he calls 'The Red Bead Experiment.' I once attended a seminar about Deming's management theories and the presenter demonstrated the Red Bead Experiment for the audience. It was very funny.

"He announced to the audience that he was starting a new department and he needed six 'willing workers.' Six people in the audience volunteered. He then showed them an aquarium filled with 4000 beads—a mixture of red and white beads. 20 percent of the beads were red.

"The product this department made was to be a cup of fifty beads. The process was for each willing worker to stir the mixture of beads, put on a blindfold and scoop up fifty beads with the cup. They were told that the customer would not accept any red beads among the fifty. Before handing in their sample to be presented, they were required to count the red beads they had scooped up.

"The presenter then made a chart showing the performance of the workers." At that point Larry drew a little chart on his pad.

Name	Number of Red Beads Produced
Mike	9
Pete	5
Terry	12
Jack	4
Louise	10
Gary	8
Total	*51*

"After all six willing workers attempted to make samples with zero red beads, the presenter reviewed their performance. 'Not bad for a first try' said the presenter. 'Jack, I am particularly impressed with your performance. And Pete, you too did a good job for a first try. Terry, I'm worried about you. Let's try again but this time I'm going to give a company tee shirt to the worker who produces zero red beads."

"They try again, and post the results.

Name	Number of Red Beads Produced	Number of Red Beads Produced
Mike	9	8
Pete	5	15
Terry	12	8
Jack	4	2
Louise	10	11
Gary	8	9
Total	*51*	*53*

"'Jack, you are doing fantastic. Keep up the good work' announces the presenter. 'Terry, I'm happy to see that you're making an attempt to improve. But as you all know, our customer will not accept any red beads. I think I'll need to retrain each of you.' The presenter then demonstrates how to stir the bead mixture in the aquarium, how to put on the blindfold and how to dip the cup into the mixture.

"They try once again.

Name	Number of Red Beads Produced	Number of Red Beads Produced	Number of Red Beads Produced
Mike	9	8	15
Pete	5	15	13
Terry	12	8	9
Jack	4	2	1
Louise	10	11	13
Gary	8	9	3
Total	*51*	*53*	*54*

"'I am very disappointed in this team. I offered Tee shirts as an incentive and I took the time to re-train you. Pete and Louise,

I don't know why you can't be as good as Jack. Pete and Louise…YOU'RE FIRED!

"'I think for this next time I'm going to add an inspector to this team. Each of you will deliver your samples to the inspector and he will personally count the red beads for you.'

"They tried for a fourth time.

Name	Number of Red Beads Produced	Number of Red Beads Produced	Number of Red Beads Produced	Number of Red Beads Produced
Mike	9	8	15	13
Terry	12	8	9	15
Jack	4	2	1	9
Gary	8	9	3	1
Total	51	53	54	38

"'Jack, what happened to you?' asked the presenter. 'You were doing great. And what's the matter with you Mike and you Terry. Didn't you see what I did to Pete and Louise? Didn't I add an inspector to help you? Mike and Terry - YOU'RE FIRED!

"And they tried one last time.

Name	Number of Red Beads Produced	Number of Red Beads Produced	Number of Red Beads Produced	Number of Red Beads Produced	Number of Red Beads Produced
Jack	4	2	1	9	15
Gary	8	9	3	1	15
Total	51	53	54	38	30

"'Jack, Gary what the hell is wrong with you two?' shouts the presenter. 'I've tried incentives, I've tried more training, I added an inspector, and I showed you the consequence of poor performance. Jack and Gary—YOU'RE FIRED!'"

Larry continued, "It was a very entertaining demonstration but it made an important point. Our employees typically do the best with what they are given. They truly are willing workers. But sometimes we give them processes with red beads in them. The red beads could be the flawed process he was given, or the people he works with, or his equipment, or his customers, or his supervision, or his noisy, confusing, uncomfortable environment. So maybe the stars in the organization really aren't stars at all. Maybe we gave them processes without any red beads in them."

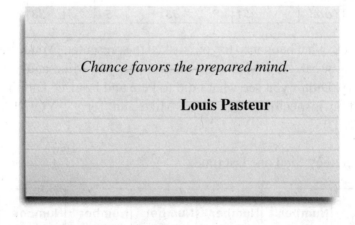

Chance favors the prepared mind.

Louis Pasteur

Chapter 21
The Visitors

Janet Kass was working at her desk when her phone rang. Brady was on the line.

"Janet, I need you to come down here in thirty minutes. Don Esters just called me from his cell phone. He's on his way here for a surprise visit and he's boiling mad. Our customers have been calling him about our late deliveries and long lead times and he wants to know what we're doing about it."

Don Esters is Sonic's CEO—Brady's boss. It was very unusual for him to just drop by for a surprise visit to the facility so Janet knew something was up. When Janet arrived at Brady's office suite, his secretary said it was okay for Janet to just go in. As she approached Brady's office door to open it, she could hear Don Esters shouting at Brady. It was clear that Brady was receiving a dressing down from his boss.

Janet knocked on the door and was asked to come in by Brady. Both men were red-faced. Esters knew Janet and gave her a polite greeting. She was well prepared. "Hello there Mr. Esters, good to see you. I understand the topic for today is lead times and late deliveries. I think I have some very good news for you. We have recently initiated a program to implement a Lean Enterprise and are hard at work removing the waste from all our processes. Not just in the factory but throughout."

Esters then turned to Jim Brady. "Jim, I've been here half an hour talking with you. Why didn't you mention the work you're doing with Lean?"

Janet Kass didn't give Brady a chance to reply. She interjected, "Mr. Esters, come with us to the cafeteria. Our Lean Promotions Office maintains a bulletin board there showing all our employees the Lean work in progress."

Janet and the two men walked down the long hallway to the cafeteria with Janet a few steps in front of Esters and Brady who were still engaged in a conversation of their own. Although they were speaking quietly she could hear snatches of what was being said. She heard Brady say something about how much lower the labor rates were in China. She then heard Esters reply, "Jim I don't know why you are so focused on this China thing. Don't you ask yourself how can it be that so many U.S. manufacturers still survive, or even thrive, despite the high labor costs in our country?"

She led the two men to the bulletin board in the cafeteria and explained the flow charts depicting the improved processes for order fulfillment and the list of active projects.

Janet explained "One thing we haven't shown yet on the bulletin boards is how much money we are saving with our Lean initiatives. So far we're up to about $300,000 and we've just started. Our focus is on lead time reduction and the elimination of non-value added work from our office areas. We are transforming this company and doing it fast. We know that Jim is interested in outsourcing because it may be an opportunity to reduce our costs by 20 percent. We think we can save more than 20 percent and improve our lead times without the need to outsource all our production."

Brady didn't have a clue what he was looking at on the bulletin boards but was very grateful for what Janet was doing. Don Esters put his arm around Jim Brady. "Jim, I think this work is sensational. I see you know where you are now, you know where you want to be, you know what your impediments are, and you know what you're going to do about them."

Janet left the two men and returned to the office knowing that she had shoved a gold nugget under Brady's nose.

Later that afternoon, Janet's phone rang and she could see on the screen that Brady was calling her. "Janet, I really appreciate what you did for me this morning with Esters. I'm sorry to bother you, but I need your help again. This is turning out to be the worst day I can remember. I just got a call from Allen Schulman, the CEO of the Spectrum Group. He's in his car on his way over here and wants to talk about our lead times. Just what I needed today—getting yelled at by Schulman, our biggest customer. I would like you to give him the same run-through you gave Esters. I'll call you when we're ready."

About forty minutes later, Janet was summoned into Brady's office. It was one of those déjà vu moments. As she reached for the doorknob of Brady's office, she could hear Schulman yelling. When she entered the room she could see that both men were red-faced. Brady was getting hammered.

Allen Schulman and Janet knew one another. "Good to see you, Allen" Janet said as she shook his hand in greeting. "I bet you've been talking to Jim about lead times. Please come with me to a display in our cafeteria where I can explain what we're doing about lead time improvements."

Janet Kass gave Allen Schulman the same explanation she had just given Don Esters that morning. She concluded by saying, "I know you're frustrated, Allen, but I hope you can see that we're attacking all our key problem areas with a company-wide focus. Everyone in this building is now engaged in making this company Lean. We're using Kaizen as our main tool."

"That's amazing," replied Allen Schulman. "Because three months ago we were acquired by a huge corporation and they mandate that all their divisions become Lean. We've had people from their corporate headquarters living with us for the past three months. We spend a lot of time on Kaizen and I think it's fantastic.

"I must say I'm leaving here in a better mood than the one I came here with. But I need to see those lead times improve if you want to keep doing business with me."

Every job is a self-portrait.
Autograph your work with excellence.

Anon

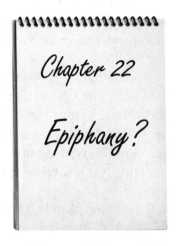

Chapter 22

Epiphany?

Jim Brady had assembled his staff to discuss the move to China. He started the meeting by telling them about how Janet Kass rescued him from Allen the day before. He said that by showing Allen that we were using Lean techniques to improve delivery performance, we probably saved the account. He also mentioned that he went back to the bulletin board in the cafeteria by himself and was very impressed with all the Lean work that was going on. "Maybe he discovered more gold nuggets," Larry thought.

"Jim, I have an idea about how to speed up this transition to China" said Larry. "This transition period is going to be massively complex. And after the transition we will need to have in place the infrastructure to manage this new extended supply chain. We don't need to reinvent the wheel. Why don't we pay a visit to the Apache plant that is being run by my friend Bob Simms, whom you all know.

"His company went through the transition three years ago. We can learn from his mistakes and copy the infrastructure processes he uses to control his Chinese suppliers. I'm sure he would agree to let us spend a morning over there."

"Sounds good to me," said Jim. "I would love to see the operation he set up to deal with China. 'Steal shamelessly' is one of my favorite sayings. You're right Larry, no point in reinventing the wheel. See what you can do about setting up a field trip to Apache." Jim Brady stood up behind his desk— his signal that the meeting had just ended.

Larry called Bob at the Apache plant and arranged for Simms to give them a talk the next morning about outsourcing to China. The next morning Larry was driving the company's nine-passenger van to bring Jim and his staff over to the Apache plant fifteen miles away.

The Apache reception lobby was quite large with a number of impressive display cabinets showing the company's bicycle components. The thing that struck the Sonic Speaker staff was the high spirits of the Apache employees who were in the lobby as they entered. They didn't see that kind of good mood over at Sonic.

After signing in the visitors, the receptionist called Bob Simms, who shortly came bounding into the lobby with a big smile and hearty greeting. He also took a minute to say good morning to the two receptionists who then teased Simms about his haircut.

On the way to the Apache conference room, they passed through a section of the factory. Both Larry and Jim had seen the factory three years ago. At that time, Bob had gotten Larry interested in Lean but Larry couldn't convince his boss to go in that direction. As a strategy, Simms invited Brady to see the Apache plant and how their Lean initiatives had made the company amazingly successful. It was that trip that convinced Brady to allow Smith to bring Lean into the Sonic factory. Unfortunately, Lean didn't spread past the Sonic factory.

The Sonic staff was very impressed with what they saw of the Apache factory, even though they only caught a glimpse of it as they were walking to the conference room. As they made their way through the office corridors on the way to the conference room, they were struck with all the displays of metrics.

Many of the bulletin boards were dedicated to recent Kaizen event successes and others to Apache general metrics, metrics such as: on-time delivery, backlog, customer satisfaction, customer lead time, warrantee expense, and sales dollars. This information was simply not available to Sonic employees.

Bob was leading the Sonic people down the corridor when he stopped at the entrance of the finance office. Next to the entrance was a bulletin board. Simms pointed to the bulletin board and addressed the group. "I want to mention something about our metrics. When we kicked off our Lean program about four years ago, our focus was strictly in the factory. We were astonished to learn at that time that about 25 percent of the things we did there were MUDA—non-value added activities.

"We were able to remove a lot of that MUDA through a number of Kaizen events but we were disappointed that very few of the improvements made it to the bottom line. We were seriously considering outsourcing everything to China.

"We did a great job of removing waste from our factory but did nothing to the office functions that supported our factory. We had lots of metrics of our factory functions but not one of our administrative areas. And that's when we set a goal of having more than a Lean factory—we wanted a Lean Enterprise. Once we started to do Kaizen events in the offices we were astonished to learn that as much as 75 percent of the efforts there were not adding any value.

"Now every administrative function is working on getting leaner and leaner. That's what these bulletin boards outside the office areas show. On this board the finance department is showing its improvement chart on the time it takes to do the month-end close. When they started the project with a Kaizen event it was taking them five days. Now as you can see they got it down to one and a half days.

"We keep these bulletin boards outside the offices in the corridor so that everyone in the company will know what's going on throughout the organization. We're fostering an environment where every single employee constantly asks the question, 'how can we do a better job today than we did yesterday.'"

As they made their way down the corridor they looked at all the bulletin boards. The materials office had a chart showing inventory turns. The customer service office chart showed the number of days required to deliver a spare part. All the Sonic people noticed that most of the charting was done with the same three-part format Larry had introduced to them showing trend, Pareto, and responsibilities on one 8½ x 11-inch page. Besides the surprise of seeing all the metrics on display was the surprise of how good a mood everyone seemed to be in. Things seemed to be running very smoothly—almost effortlessly—and people seemed generally cheerful.

That cheerfulness contrasted to the prevailing mood at the Sonic offices where everyone was in constant panic mode, as they seemed to be perpetually engaged in tackling the latest crisis.

Bob Simms escorted them into his conference room where a table with juice, fruit, cookies, and doughnuts was set up for the guests.

"Welcome to Apache" Bob began as the group sat down with their coffee. "I haven't prepared a formal presentation for you but I understand you want to hear about outsourcing to China. We're heavy into that now but there's a lot you can learn from errors we made.

"Three years ago, we thought that we would outsource some of our products to China. We made a mistake in the beginning—we thought all we had to do was pack up our specifications, ship them to China, and then just sit back and get our products made for 20 percent less. And that was the bill of goods our agent sold us: 'Take your specs, send them to China and start saving money.'

"We had to learn the hard way that, when you outsource, there wouldn't be any savings on day one or in month six for that matter. We didn't anticipate all the trips our staff had to make to clear up problems caused mostly by miscommunications and we certainly didn't expect the cost of all the air shipments we needed to make because of this new inflexible supply chain that had five weeks of our product in transit at any given time. Offshore outsourcing, we learned, is a long-term investment with long-term payback. The transition not only took longer than we thought, it cost a lot more as well. We didn't expect that the transition would take a full year.

"I've heard about companies who have tried to outsource to China, and nine months later they pulled the plug because they weren't saving any money.

"Another thing we didn't anticipate was the effect on morale. We never planned to move all our production to China but, because we didn't do a thorough job of explaining our plans to our workforce, we saw work slowing down. What we learned was that, if you don't spend the time explaining your plans, your employees are going to make up stories about what's happening.

"The most useful suggestion I can give you is to rely heavily on your engineering staff for vendor selection as well as during the transition process. Your engineers can tell if the vendor has the right equipment and can provide the controlled processes and consistent level of quality needed to produce reliable products.

"Many U.S. companies think that once they outsource, their hands are free and they can go on to doing other things. China product transitions, engineering revisions, root cause analysis, troubleshooting, and warrantee issues will be ongoing. You will need to set up a full time organization for these things.

"I suggest you make an appointment for your technical people to come spend a day over here with our folks who can show them what we've learned and put in place to control our Chinese suppliers.

"I'm sure by now you know that we didn't outsource all our production. That was our original intent. We only outsourced our low-end models. One of the things that led to that decision was a story we heard about Motorola. They had hired a Taiwan company to design and manufacture millions of mobile phones. But then the Taiwan company started selling similar phones under their own name. Motorola then pulled the contract.

"We couldn't afford that to happen to us. We have proprietary technology to make our bike components. Some of these techniques, like the use of synthetic diamonds in our bearings, took us decades to develop and perfect. We do them in rooms we never let visitors see. We can't afford to have somebody steal them.

"I've been to your plant and I know you also have manufacturing processes you wouldn't like your competition to learn. To be perfectly frank, I think you have rocks in your head if you outsource all your production.

"Larry's been telling me about the Lean initiatives you've got going in your administrative areas. You have terrific products, a seasoned loyal workforce, and nothing stopping you from becoming a world-class manufacturer. If you are willing to invest a year in transitioning your low-end products to China, and during that year focus your efforts on becoming a Lean

Enterprise, I think you will be able to enjoy great success."

Everyone in the van driving back to Sonic was silent. Larry wondered if Brady saw the gold nugget this time.

> *Leadership is not just the leaders demonstrating their talents, but the release of the talents of the people they lead.*
>
> **Sid Joynson**

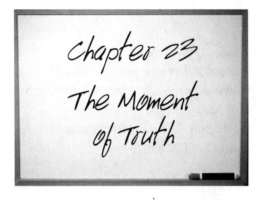

Chapter 23
The Moment
of Truth

The first thing Larry did the next morning when he got to work was to type up his letter of resignation. If the trip to Apache didn't convince Brady of the merits of focusing efforts on the elimination of waste in the administrative areas in order to create a Lean Enterprise, then he no longer wanted to work at Sonic.

After printing his resignation, Larry set off on his morning rounds of the operation, but his mind was elsewhere. His mind was on finding a new job—if it came to that. Shortly after he returned to his office, the phone rang. It was Brady asking Larry to come to his office. Larry took the letter of resignation from his desk drawer, folded it carefully, and inserted it between the pages of the note pad he carried into Brady's office.

This was the moment of truth. If Brady was going to order Larry to devote his full energies to outsourcing and therefore abandon his efforts to remove waste from the administrative areas, he was fully prepared to quit. Larry's heart was pounding as he entered Brady's office. He didn't have a clue what Brady was going to say. As he entered the office he tried to read the expression on Brady's face to anticipate the conversation that was about to happen.

Larry had fantasized how much he would enjoy working for his friend and mentor, Bob Simms. He thought that, if he quit, maybe Simms would give him a job. Or maybe Simms didn't have a place for Larry. At this point, Larry didn't care; all he knew was that he couldn't bear to remain at Sonic if he was forced to abandon his Lean efforts.

"Have a seat, Larry," Brady began. "I once read that very successful business people make up their minds very quickly and change their minds very slowly. In contrast, poor business people make up their minds very slowly and change their minds very quickly. The example of this is Henry Ford who for years only made his cars in black even though his subordinates kept advising him to offer the car in assorted colors. Ford changed his mind after many years—many highly profitable years. The demand for his cars was so high, he didn't have to offer colors.

"I'm like that; I make up my mind really fast and change it very slowly. As you know, I have been focused on moving our operations to China. I wanted to take advantage of the low labor there. It didn't occur to me until our visit to Apache that I had been comparing our current costs to labor cost there. I wasn't comparing China to what our cost and delivery performance could be if we could remove the waste from our administrative processes.

"Simms said yesterday that in the typical company 75 percent of what goes on in the administrative areas is waste. Taking the waste out of our admin areas would transform everything we do from product concept to launch, from customer order to delivery, from raw material into the arms of our customer, and then through the life cycle of all our goods and services. It would involve the efforts of everyone in product development, sales, scheduling, our accounting departments, our technical departments, and marketing. If you are right and we could get our lead times down to about two weeks and we could speed up our glacial new product introduction cycle, I think we could have a terrific company here.

"I've been distracted by my focus on China, but I'm not totally blind to what's going on with your attempts to improves the administrative functions here. This morning the first thing I did when I got here was to revisit the bulletin board in the cafeteria showing all the recent Lean achievements in our administrative areas. I think I'm ready to change my mind.

"I'll make you a deal Larry. If you agree to spearhead my project to move our low-end product to China, I'll agree to do everything I can to help make this a Lean Enterprise and will promise that I will limit our outsourcing only to our low-end line, just like they're doing at Apache.

"I want to move quickly with the China outsourcing. That will take a lot of your personal time and will certainly mean you will be taking a few trips to China in the next four months.

But you have my word that I will take a leadership role in making this company all that it can be."

Larry was speechless. Brady really did see the gold nuggets they pushed under his nose. Brady really did see what he was supposed to see at Apache. The time bomb was certainly ticking, but it just got defused.

"The trip to Apache really opened my eyes to things and got me to thinking. Sure lots of companies in America outsource to China. There are certain products we have no business making here. There's no money to be made in America sewing soccer balls or sewing shirts together. But there is money to be made in other products that America is very good at making, like computers and aircraft for commercial airlines. That's what Apache discovered when they decided to outsource only their low-end products but remain focused on developing and manufacturing their high-margin products.

"What I saw at Apache was a Lean Enterprise. It looked like everyone was involved, not just the shop floor. And it was very obvious that this came about because Bob Simms was leading the effort and he was the man at the top of their organization.

"I didn't say much on the ride back from Apache. That's because I was deep in thought about what to do next. To tell you the truth, I didn't sleep well last night. I spent most of the night thinking about what I want *us* to do.

"I think we have some very good things going for us if we want to become a Lean Enterprise. First of all, we have a crisis. You know that when a ship starts sinking it's not hard to mobilize the crew. That's because a crisis sharpens the mind and demands teamwork. I think that, when the news gets out that we are moving a high-volume product to China, people will treat that as a crisis. That's good because we will get their attention.

"The second thing we have going for us is that we have some momentum now. You have overcome a lot of initial inertia. You had excellent success in the factory and you're beginning to get good successes in our administrative areas these past few weeks.

"And the third thing we have is your establishment of the Lean Promotions Office. What we don't have going for us is leadership from the top. I'm prepared to do that. But there are things I will need from your Lean Promotions Office. One of the most important things I need is a method of keeping score. That's one of the most impressive things I saw at Apache. You know how much I like my graphs I keep on the wall of this office. I really believe that *you get what you measure*. But only people who visit my office and look at my wall know what I measure. There were metrics everywhere I looked at Apache. It's obvious that their posted metrics are a key tool for their continuous improvements.

"I'm fully prepared to take the leadership role in making this company Lean. I will rely heavily on your Lean Promotions Office to develop metrics that keep score and reward people so they will continue to do the right things. I will need your team to help establish the priorities for our Lean initiatives and to assure that every single person in this organization gets trained in Lean techniques and gets to use them."

Chapter 23

Brady then held up the legal pad that was on his desk. That pad was the only thing on Brady's immaculate desk. "Larry, look at this. I made a list of what I think my role will be in creating a Lean Enterprise. Let me tell you what I've written. I view that my main role is to promote Lean in my words and my actions. You will be able to count on me to meet frequently with your Lean Promotions Office to plan new activities and to review our progress. You can be certain that I will hold managers and supervisors accountable for implementing Lean business system activities. If you need capital, I will do what I can to get that for you. I want every single employee involved with this and I need you to give me suggestions on how I can help with that."

Larry was speechless. How could Brady have done such a turn-around?

Maybe he really did see the light? Maybe, just maybe, Brady isn't such a bad guy after all.

APPENDIX A

Glossary of Lean Terms

Concurrent Engineering – Concurrent engineering is a business strategy which replaces the traditional product development process with one in which tasks are done in parallel and there is an early consideration for every aspect of a product's development process. The objective of Concurrent Engineering is to create products which are better, cheaper, and more quickly brought to market.

Cycle Time – The *actual* time an operator takes to complete an operation.

Deming's 14 Points – W. Edwards Deming in Chapter 2 of *Out of the Crisis* (MIT Press, 2000), outlines 14 points as the basis for transformation of American industry:

1. Create constancy of purpose toward improvement of product and service with the aim to become competitive, to stay in business, and to provide jobs.

2. Adopt the new philosophy. We are in a new economic age. Western management must awaken to the challenge, must learn their responsibilities, and take on leadership for change.

3. Cease dependence on inspection to achieve quality. Eliminate the need for inspection on a mass basis by building quality into the product in the first place.

4. End the practice of awarding business on the basis of price tag. Instead, minimize total cost. Move toward a single supplier for any one item, on a long-term relationship of loyalty and trust.

5. Improve constantly and forever the system of production and service, to improve quality and productivity, and thus constantly decrease costs.

6. Institute training on the job.

7. Institute leadership. The aim of supervision should be to help people and machines and gadgets to do a better job. Supervision of management is in need of overhaul, as well as supervision of production workers.

8. Drive out fear, so that everyone may work effectively for the company.

9. Break down barriers between departments. People in research, design, sales, and production must work as a team, to foresee problems of production and in use that may be encountered with the product or service.

10. Eliminate slogans, exhortations, and targets for the work force asking for zero defects and new levels of productivity. Such exhortations only create adversarial relationships, as the bulk of the causes of low quality and low productivity belong to the system and thus lie beyond the power of the work force.

   Eliminate management by objective. Eliminate management by numbers, numerical goals. Substitute leadership.

11. Remove barriers that rob the hourly worker of his right to pride of workmanship. The respon-

sibility of supervisors must be changed from sheer numbers to quality.

12. Remove barriers that rob people in management and in engineering of their right to pride of workmanship. This means, abolishment of the annual or merit rating and of management by objective.

13. Institute a vigorous program of education and self-improvement.

14. Put everybody in the company to work to accomplish the transformation. The transformation is everybody's job.

Dr. W. Edwards Deming (1900-1993)

W. Edwards Deming was employed by AT&T at the end of World War II when he was sent to Japan to help rebuild the country. He educated Japanese industrialists in the fields of statistical research and application.

Among his many accomplishments is the funding of the Deming Prize (established by the Union of Japanese Scientists and Engineers and named in his honor) to promote the continued development of quality control in Japan.

Flow – The progression of a product along the value stream with no stoppages or rework.

Internal Customer – A downstream process, or an individual requesting work or service. Since internal customers don't pay for goods or services, anything they request in addition to value added tasks is waste.

Just in Time – The JIT production system originated at the Toyota Motor Company by Taiichi Ohno. Simply stated, it is a method of delivering the right quantity of the right part at the right time.

Kaizen – Literally translated as *continuous improvement*. With Kaizen, progress is made with numerous incremental ideals, as opposed to one fix-it-all alternative. This runs counter to the American tendency toward bold moves and great leaps.

Kaizen Event – Dramatic focused improvement exercise in a service or production operation in a very short period of time. The objective of the event is to discover and eliminate waste.

Kanban – Japanese word meaning *signal*. It typically is a card attached to a bin of parts. The card is used to signal upstream production processes that a replenishment point has been reached and that a certain number of parts must now be delivered to a designated location.

Lead Time – The time the customer has to wait after placing an order.

Lagging Indicators – Metrics that describe performance at some point, or over some duration, in the past. These metrics are often calculated at the end of a day, or a week, to show shop performance over the course of that day, or that week.

The good thing about using lagging metrics is that they can be made very accurate, and several metrics can be overlaid on the same graph to show interactions. The downside of their use is that lagging indicators get to you too late. You can't do anything about last month's poor performance.

Leading Indicators – Metrics that predict future performance. Leading metrics can be applied to jobs that are currently in WIP to predict performance at the time those jobs are shipped out. Leading metrics can also be applied to jobs that are not yet in WIP to predict what shop performance will be when those jobs arrive, or when those jobs are shipped out in turn.

The benefits of using leading metrics are that adjustments can be made to operations before a problem arises. The downside of using leading metrics is that they are only projections.

Lean – The term comes to us from Japan and was first described to Americans in a book published in 1990 called *The Machine That Changed the World.* In this book by authors James Womack, Daniel Jones, and Daniel Roos, describe Japanese management practices that enabled their stunning success in the automotive and consumer electronics businesses.

When "Lean" companies are compared to ordinary companies, we see these differences:

- Lean companies take *one-half* the human effort

- Lean companies have one-half the defects in the finished product (or service)

- Lean companies require one-third the engineer-ing effort

- Lean companies use one-half the floor space for

the same output

- Lean companies have 90 percent less inventory

Simply put, "Lean" means the establishment and improvement of flow principally through the identification and elimination of waste and the continual reduction of required resources.

MRP – Material Requirements Planning was developed initially in the 1970's. MRP is a method to determine material purchase requirements (when, how much) based on lead times and quantity discounts.

MRPII – Manufacturing Resource Planning evolved from MRP by combining "capacity planning" models with MRP models. These "capacity planning' models use quality and lead time data to plan order releases to the shop floor.

ERP – Enterprise Resource Planning has extended MRPII to all business functions, and also encompasses supply chain management principles.

It is often said that MRP/MRPII/ERP are "push" systems, and are therefore incompatible with Lean production principles. The truth is that MRP/MRPII/ERP systems are wonderful "information" systems, and can be quite compatible with Lean systems, as long as they aren't used to drive production through "push" methods.

MUDA – Waste. All of "Lean" is centered on the identification and elimination of waste, in all its various forms. Understanding the nature of waste is the first step in being able to recognize it, and thereby work to eliminate it.

NVA – Non-Value Added – Those tasks the customer isn't willing to (or does not want to) pay for.

NVAE – Non-Value Added, but Essential. The payroll department, for example adds no value to the customer but all employees will agree that the department is certainly necessary. These NVA tasks must be performed because:

- Current processes or systems require the tasks to be performed

- Processes or systems require redesign before the tasks can be eliminated

- There is a specific customer requirement (such as a required inspection)

Ohno, Taiicho (1912-1990)

As a Production Engineer and Assembly Manager for Toyota (in the 1940s and 1950s), Ohno collaborated with Shigeo Shingo to develop the Toyota Production System. Ohno became an Executive Vice President at Toyota in 1975. In developing the Toyota Production System, Ohno often credited both Henry Ford and American supermarkets for his accomplishments with production flow and Just-In-Time techniques.

Operation – A set of steps performed at a particular workstation.

Process – A series of steps required to create an end result. Each process has an input and an output. The process could produce a service, a design, an answer to a customer, a step along an assembly line or a complete product.

The terms "process" and "operation" are used interchangeably. However, in a *Lean* context, the distinction is an important one. Lean seeks to improve the flow of the entire process, as opposed to "maximizing" the output of each operation.

Pull – The movement of a product from downstream to upstream. The pull is created by customer demand rather than from a central scheduling point.

In a "pull" system (as opposed to traditional "push" systems), flow is restricted to actual downstream requirements.

Pull production keeps WIP inventory to a minimum which not only reduces space requirements but labor requirements as well. Additionally, quality issues are much easier to detect in pull systems which can have a significant effect on defect rates.

Push – Output based on capacity (regardless of demand).

In a "push" system, each work center produces to its capacity regardless of downstream requirements.

Quality Function Deployment (QFD) – A decision-making process for multi-skilled project teams which develops a common understanding of the voice of the customer and a consensus on the final specifications of a product or service.

Sensei – A master or teacher.

Shingo, Shigeo (1909-1990)

Dr. Shigeo Shingo was the architect of many of the tools of the Toyota Production System (i.e., Lean production). The Shingo Prize for Excellence in Manufacturing was established in 1988 by Utah State University, to promote awareness of Lean manufacturing concepts and recognize companies in the United States, Canada, and Mexico that achieve world-class manufacturing status. Also in 1988, Utah State University awarded Shingo an honorary Doctorate in Business, recognizing his contributions in the areas of Lean and World-class Manufacturing.

Spaghetti Diagram – Also called a *dance chart*. A sketch showing the path a part or person takes through the steps of production. It is called a spaghetti diagram because it looks like a plate of spaghetti.

Takt Time – The rate of production that matches the actual customer requirements. It is calculated by dividing the available time in a day by the daily customer demand.

Value – From a Lean perspective, "value" is anything a paying customer is willing to pay for. Anything a customer is not willing to pay for is considered MUDA (waste) and should be designed out of processes. Just because customers are "required" to pay for waste (due to pricing) doesn't mean they are 'willing' to pay for it.

Value Stream – The activities required to provide a customer with a final product. The activities begin with product conception and end with the delivery of the product to the end customer.

Value Stream Map – A graphic depiction of the value stream. The map is a sketch that shows such details as cycle times, inventory levels, and communication routes.

Waste – An activity performed in a process that does not add value to the output of the process. See MUDA.

WIP – Work in Process. In the UK, it's called Work in Progress.

APPENDIX B

Lean Enterprise Assessment Forms*

*Electronic copies of these forms are available on cd or by e-mail. Please contact us at info@wcmfg.com or 260-637-8064

Appendix B

Lean Enterprise Assessment		

Baseline Report Card (Your initial impression)

The levels of LEAN implementation are expressed below.
Most organizations fall within one of the following categories.

Check ✓ the box that you think describes your LEAN GRADE.

Lean Implementation Grade	Definition	✔
A	We implemented LEAN to a superior extent. LEAN is now part of the culture. Results are of world class or industry benchmark status. Management has incentives to keep it running.	
B	We made a strong effort. Implementation has produced visible gains in the organization. Completing implementation is a clear priority and adequate resources are applied. Management tracks performance.	
C	We are in implementation phases and getting minimal benefit. Senior Management has allocated resources and is monitoring progress	
D	We're trying to get started, but effort is in its infancy. Only one department is doing LEAN work. Management allocated some resources but not enough.	
D-	No more than pilot implementation. We talk about it but don't do it much. No interest by Senior Management.	
F	It hasn't been addressed by the organization. Maintaining the status quo is supported.	

248

Use the following scoring scale when filling out this detailed survey

1 = NO implementation of the item; it has NOT been ADDRESSED by the organization

2 = To a very LITTLE extent; very LITTLE AWARENESS of the item in the organization

3 = To a MODERATE extent; the item is in the MIDDLE of being ADDRESSED

4 = To a LARGE extent; the item has been ADDRESSED and DATA on RESULTS is AVAILABLE

5= To a GREAT extent; the item is fully IMPLEMENTED and COMPLETE RESULTS are AVAILABLE

Part 1 – Lean Organizational Environment

1A. Top Management Support	1 - 5
To what extent has top management (including CEO, President, VPs, General Managers, Directors, etc.) exhibited support for lean business systems:	
1. They (GM and Senior Staff) understand the concepts of Lean and have some understanding of world-class performance in Lean	
2. They visibly promote Lean Business Systems in words and actions	
3. They commit time to planning for lean business system activities and reviewing progress	
4. They hold their managers and supervisors accountable for implementing lean business system activities and make that part of the formal review process	
5. They recognize managers and employees for lean business systems initiatives and continuous improvement innovations	
6.They invest resources (including capital and people's time) to identify and implement lean business system initiatives	
7. They encourage or mandate that employees at all levels be involved and participate in lean business systems initiatives	
8. They regularly visit areas where the work gets done – production, purchasing, receiving, stockroom, shipping, warehouse, lunchrooms, accounting, etc.	
9. They regularly participate in Lean activities, including reviews, walkthroughs, strategic planning and celebrations	
10. They have a vision and that vision is clear to everyone. There are qualitative expectations of improvement goals by management that define critical success factors for the next 90 days	
11. They have the required communication with and alignment of union and managament objectives (if a unionized facillity)	
Add 1 through 11 →	**Score 1A.**

Appendix B

1B. Organizational Buy-in and Support	1 - 5
Rate the understanding and regular practices of LEAN operations (Identifying waste, simplifying, visual controls, etc) in each of the following groups:	
1. The employee population in general	
2. The hourly population hierarchy	
3. The manufacturing organization	
4. The engineering organization	
5. The maintenance organization	
6. The production planning and scheduling organization	
7. The purchasing organization	
8. The management support organization (including accounting, HR, etc.)	
9. Senior Management – GM/CEO and section heads	
Add 1 through 9 →	**Score 1B.**

1C. Employee Involvement	1 - 5
To what extent has there been involvement of employees through:	
1. Cross-functional teams participate in Kaizen events	
2. Hourly personnel participate in Kaizen events	
3. Establishment of cross-functional steering group or review body for the lean business system approach	
Add 1 through 3 →	**Score 1C.**

1D. Organizational Alignment	1 - 5
How effectively has the organization dealt with:	
1. Employee concerns for job security relating to the elimination of waste	
2. Employee concerns about rewards and recognition for lean business systems involvement	
3. Establishing a philosophy or policy statement that articulates what the organization is trying to accomplish with the lean business systems approach	
4. Promoting an environment of continuous improvement with a never-ending quest for waste elimination	
5. Routinely celebrating gains made by LEAN initiatives.	
6. Promoting continuous learning and skill building at all levels of the organization	
Add 1 through 6 →	**Score 1D.**

1E. Problem Solving and Continuous Improvement	1 - 5
To what extent have the following tools and techniques been implemented:	
1. Communication (i.e. a Lean Kickoff Meeting) and Lean training	
2. Kaizen / Continuous Improvement workshops	
3. Process Improvement / Process Mapping	
4. Basic problem solving tools (includes brainstorming, Fishbone, pareto diagrams, histograms, graphs, checksheets, Is/Is Not, Kepner Tregoe)	
5. Statistical Process Control (SPC)	
6. Benchmarking of best practices	
7. Taguchi methods / design of experiments (DOE)	
8. Suggestion systems	
9. Continuous improvement teams / work group teams	
Add 1 through 9 →	Score 1E.

1F. How Metrics are Used	1 - 5
To what extent are metrics used for improvement:	
1. By upper management not just to set improvement targets but to help the company achieve its organizational goals	
2. By middle management/supervision to focus resources and activities for departmental improvement	
3. By the workforce to gauge their performance and suggest areas for improvement. Metrics therefore are conspicuously posted throughout the enterprise.	
4. As feedstock to problem solving / continuous improvement teams for setting baselines and determining the scope of their issue	
5. As a communication tool to the organization to show progress on continuous improvement	
6. Used to measure what is really important. Company metrics conform to the old saying, *"A Few metrics in the hands of many, instead of many metrics in the hands of a few."*	
Add 1 through 6 →	Score 1F.

1G. Lean Administration	1 - 5
To what extent has Lean thinking improved the office and technical processes?	
1. The company is aligned by value streams	
2. There are global systems metrics in place that measure the enterprise - not just local departmental functions	
3. Accounting and Manufacturing agree on the company metrics	
4. Office Kaizen events are routine	
5. Offices have been arranged in cells	
6. Offices have Lean measurement systems in place	
7. Office information product lead times are measured and have been reduced successfully	
Add 1 through 7 →	Score 1G.

Part 2 – Lean Manufacturing (If applicable)

2A. Supplier Management System	1 - 5
To what extent have the following systems been implemented?	
1. A system for supplier involvement and development	
2. A strategy that translates the organization's business plan into supply base requirements	
4. A system for identifying key suppliers and rationalizing the supplier base	
5. A system for accurately and fairly measuring subcontractor performance	
6. A system for accurately and fairly measuring TOTAL supplier performance	
7. A system for assuring subcontractor investment in lean systems and continuous improvement	
8. More than 50% of items purchase (by value) are single sourced	
9. Materials management's effectiveness is visible via a sales, production, inventory planning process	
10. Most raw materials and purchased items come from qualified suppliers with no need for incoming inspection	
11. Most raw materials and purchased items are delivered directly to the point of use without inspection or storage	
Add 1 through 11 →	**Score 2A.**

2B. Production System	1 - 5
To what extent have the following systems been implemented?	
1. A pull system for customer orders	
2. A material handling system for material flow through production	
3. A Kanban system for work in process	
4. A Kanban system for external suppliers	
5. LEAN concepts such as "Takt time" and "Value Streams" used in the production system design	
6. A cell system to create one-piece flow	
7. Operators perform standard work. Standard work instructions are conspicuously posted	
7. Batch sizes have been absolutely minimized wherever possible	
Add 1 through 7 →	**Score 2B.**

2C. Layout and Housekeeping	1 - 5
To what extent does the layout:	
1. Exhibit 5S discipline? There's a place for everything and everything is in its place.	
2. Create a spotless, neat, safe and tidy appearance? Aisles are clearly marked.	
3. Create an environment where a stranger could walk through the plant and identify the processes and sequences as well as the current state of the operation?	
4. Use visual signaling to control flow and guide work?	
5. Have items labeled? All labels are neat and easy to read.	
6. Use color-coding as a tool to assist in doing things right?	
7. Of machines and equipment minimize the distances between sequential operations?	
Add 1 through 7 →	Score 2C.

2D. Maintenance Systems	1 - 5
To what extent has the maintenance system created:	
1. Unplanned maintenance rarely happening?	
2. A maintenance schedule for all production machinery?	
3. A method for evaluating maintenance performance and adjusting preventive maintenance activities?	
Add 1 through 3 →	Score 2D.

2E. Setups	1 - 5
To what extent are:	
1. Average setups for major equipment under nine minutes?	
2. Most machine operators trained in rapid setup techniques?	
3. Managers and workers measured and judged on setup performance?	
Add 1 through 3 →	Score 2E.

Appendix B

2F. Scheduling System	1 - 5
To what extent have the following systems been implemented?	
1. A system for level and balanced schedules for production	
2. A system for evaluating schedule performance and adjusting schedules when product mix changes	
3. A system to alter the production rate +/- 15%	
4. A system to assure that most work in process flows directly from one operation to the next without intermediate storage	
5. A system where most work in process is under Kanban	
6. A system that results in very high on time delivery performance	
7. A system that measures lead-time	
8. A system that ensures that production is in sync with demand	
9. A system where capacity is planned closer to 70% of average peak demand rather than over 90%.	
10. A system where one-piece flow is typical in most operations and product flow is synchronized to Takt time	
Add 1 through 10 ➜	**Score 2F.**

2G. New Product Planning and Development System	1 - 5
To what extent have the following systems been implemented?	
1. A system for supplier involvement in design and product planning activities	
2. A system for soliciting and reacting to supplier input for product changes and enhancements	
3. A system for the cross functional involvement in design and product planning activities	
4. A system for soliciting and reacting to operational input for product changes and enhancements	
5. A mechanism for customer involvement in design and product planning activities	
6. A program to reduce the time to bring a product to market	
Add 1 through 6 ➜	**Score 2G.**

2H. Information Systems	1 - 5
To what extent have the following systems been implemented?	
1. A cohesive system for electronic communication and data sharing with customers.	
2. A cohesive system for electronic communication and data sharing with suppliers.	
3. A shop floor data collection and dissemination system that supports material flow and the JIT system.	
4. A management information system that supports performance analysis and management decision-making.	
5. A system that supports the quality planning requirements.	
Add 1 through 5 →	Score 2H.

2I. Internal Performance Metrics	1 - 5
To what extent are the following world-class metrics achieved?	
1. On time delivery >98%	
2. First pass yield >95%	
3 Scrap and rework as a % of sales <1%	
4 Customer reject rate on shipped product <1500 ppm	
5. Total annual inventory turns > 9 times.	
Add 1 through 5 →	Score 2I.

2J. External Performance Metrics	1 - 5
To what extent are the following performance metrics being collected?	
1. Parts per million defective	
2. On-time delivery	
3. Customer returns for admin errors (order error, shipping error)	
4 Customer returns for quality problem (damaged, does not work)	
5. Customer satisfaction ratings	
6. Warrantee costs as a percentage of sales	
7. Customer reject rate of shipped product	
Add 1 through 7 →	Score 2J.

Lean Enterprise Scores
Calculated Report Card - Current State

Part 1 - Lean Organizational Environment

Category	Max Score Possible	Your Score	Percent
1A. Top Management Support	55		%
1B. Organizational Buy in and Support	45		%
1C. Employee Involvement	15		%
1D. Organizational Alignment	30		%
1E. Problem Solving / Continuous Improvement	45		%
1F. How Metrics are Used	30		%
1G. Lean Administration	35		%
Part 1 TOTALS	255		%

Part 2 - Lean Manufacturing

Category	Max Score Possible	Your Score	Percent
2A. Supplier Management Systems	55		%
2B. Production Systems	35		%
2C. Layout and Housekeeping	35		%
2D. Maintenance Systems	15		%
2E. Setups	15		%
2F. Scheduling	50		%
2G. New Product Introduction Systems	30		%
2H. Information Systems	35		%
2I. Internal Performance Metrics	30		%
2J. External Performance Metrics	25		%
Part 2 TOTALS	325		%

Index

Index

R

Rhodes, John H. 186
Roberts, Tony 114
Rocks in the Stream 101, 102
Roosevelt, Franklin D. 108
Rother, Mike 130
Rudolf, Wilma 32

S

Sarandon, Susan 132
Schweitzer, Albert 76
Sensei 139
  Definition 243
Shingo, Shigeo 243–244
Shook, John 130
Spaghetti Diagram 52, 53, 66, 69, 103, 128. *See also* Dance Chart
  Definition 244
Standardization 155–156

T

Takt Time
  Definition 244
The Machine That Changed the World 13
Time Study 52. *See also* Waste Elimination Time and Motion Study
Total Process Thinking 165
Total Supplier Costs 39–42
Tovey, C. 202
Toyota Production System 78
Trend Chart 120, 124

V

Value
  Definition 244
Value Stream
  Definition 244
Value Stream Map 130-133, 138, 142
  10 Minute Oil Change 131
  Definition 245

About The Author

JERRY FEINGOLD is a highly sought after management consultant, helping his clients become more competitive by applying Lean principles to their enterprises. He conducts major work in the United States and Europe with a wide variety of companies including manufacturers, financial services providers, and medical clinics.

He began independent consulting in 1998 after retiring from industry where he worked for thirty-four years in senior executive positions at four Fortune 100 companies. He started Continuous Improvement Consultancy in Ventura, California, helping companies improve their operations through the elimination of waste in the factory as well as the service and administrative areas.

Originally an industrial engineer (he holds a BS in Industrial Engineering and an MBA), he rose to the executive level where he conducted numerous successful domestic and international start-ups and turnarounds. While employed in industry, he became an enthusiastic practitioner of Kaizen and other Japanese Lean management techniques that he studied in Japan and applied there. In addition to numerous speaking engagements at colleges and universities, Jerry has been featured on public television and talk radio.

Lean Administration is Jerry Feingold's second book. The first book, *Getting Lean*, focuses on improving factory performance. This latest book, which describes the application of Lean to the entire enterprise, contains specific, proven, valuable tools and secrets that will assist an enterprise in reaching new levels of productivity and continuously improving.